THE PIANO QUARTET AND QUINTET

The Piano Quartet and Quintet

Style, Structure, and Scoring

BASIL SMALLMAN

CLARENDON PRESS · OXFORD
1994

Oxford University Press, Walton Street, Oxford OX2 6DP
Oxford New York
Athens Auckland Bangkok Bombay
Calcutta Cape Town Dar es Salaam Delhi
Florence Hong Kong Istanbul Karachi
Kuala Lumpur Madras Madrid Melbourne
Mexico City Nairobi Paris Singapore
Taipei Tokyo Toronto
and associated companies in
Berlin Ibadan

Oxford is a trade mark of Oxford University Press

Published in the United States
by Oxford University Press Inc., New York

British Library Cataloguing in Publication Data
Data available

Library of Congress Cataloging in Publication Data
Smallman, Basil.
    The piano quartet and quintet: style, structure, and scoring /
Basil Smallman.
    Includes bibliographical references.
    1. Piano quartets—History and criticism.   2. Piano quintets—
History and criticism.   I. Title.
ML1165.S59   1994   785'.2194—dc20   94-9685
ISBN 0-19-816374-6

1 3 5 7 9 10 8 6 4 2

Typeset by Best-set Typesetter Ltd., Hong Kong
Printed in Great Britain
on acid-free paper by
Biddles Ltd.
Guildford & King's Lynn

To Nicole
my latest grandchild

Preface

As its main title implies, this book is concerned primarily with works for the standard quartet and quintet ensembles, with piano and strings. However, no strict limitation is placed upon the range of the genres under survey, and where appropriate, reference is made to compositions which embrace larger or more varied resources. This is particularly the case in the final chapter where attention is focused on 'mixed-ensemble' works of twentieth-century origin, in which wind instruments are combined with the strings and piano, with the involvement in some cases of as many as seven performers. At the same time, since the number of works in these categories is far too large to be handled comprehensively within the limited space available, detailed consideration is reserved for what may be called the 'cornerstones' of the repertoire, while less prominent compositions, of passing relevance to the discussion, are introduced on an *ad hoc* basis, and in more general terms.

In surveying this extensive range of music I have taken a broadly historical viewpoint, but have made no attempt at a complete history. The aim has been rather to explore, in a wide-ranging manner, the overall concept of large-scale chamber composition with piano, especially in relation to structure and scoring, and to other aspects of technique. Such an approach has necessarily involved a considerable amount of descriptive analysis, and to assist with this a number of music examples are provided. But in order to reach a fuller grasp of the matters under discussion, the reader is advised to avail himself, wherever possible, of scores and recordings of the works under review—which in the case of the principal works at least, are usually readily available from libraries.

A youthful experience, turning pages for the pianist in a performance of Brahms's A major Piano Quartet, Op. 26, engendered in me a love of chamber music which, sixty years later, while no doubt less uncritical, has remained quite undiminished. Writing about music is almost certainly a more lowly pursuit than performing, composing, or even simply listening to it with deep concentration. But if, by what I have written here, some small part of my long-sustained enthusiasm is transmitted to the reader, this book will have well justified the not inconsiderable labours that have gone into it.

I am most grateful to the staff of the West Sussex County Library in Chichester for their help in securing a wide variety of study material for me, and to the Librarian of the University of Southampton for permission to consult collections held there. Amongst the many individuals who have provided me with generous assistance, I would like in particular to thank Professor Robert Orledge, Mr W. H. Fox, Dr Ernest Warburton, Professor Ludwig Finscher, and Mr David Blackwell and Miss Annette Orzel at the Oxford University Press, who have proved a constant source of wise encouragement.

Edition A.G., Vienna; William Walton, Piano Quartet, © 1976, Oxford University Press. Hugh Wood, Quintet, © 1967, Chester Music Ltd.

B.S.

November 1993

Contents

1
The Origins to 1800

By comparison with the steadfast course of development charted by Haydn and his contemporaries for the string quartet during the second half of the eighteenth century, the progress of chamber music with obbligato keyboard appears, from a present-day standpoint at least, to have been slow and irresolute. By the early 1770s the string quartet had already gained (notably with Haydn's Op. 17 and Op. 20 sets) many of the features which were eventually to mark its maturity, including four-movement structures, closely-wrought sonata schemes, and a large degree of instrumental parity. The keyboard chamber music of the period, on the other hand, though wide in range and large in quantity, usually involved only two or three movements, and, with many problems of texture and scoring still to be resolved, was often limited both in style and structure.

It is important, however, to recognize the very different circumstances, social as well as artistic, under which the two genres evolved. Whereas the string quartet (together with other stable groupings for strings alone) comprised matching instruments of potentially perfect blend, and thus provided for the ambitious composer a medium of immense scope, the keyboard ensemble, with no settled composition, and little certainty of precise balance between its constituent parts, offered an altogether less ample range of possibilities. As a result, two parallel but largely contrasted repertoires developed—one centred on the string quartet, which, with its demand for fine technique and high musical intelligence, was aimed mainly at the professional string players of the time; and the other, in which the principal burden rested on a keyboard player, with the strings confined to a simple accompanying role, which was directed chiefly at amateurs, enabling them to take part in ensemble music without over-taxing their abilities.[1] And since these amateurs belonged usually to the

[1] With reference to some sonatas by J. B. Vanhall, an anonymous reviewer in the Hamburg *Magazin der Musik*, ii (1786), 924, observed: 'In fair judgement of

nobility, or to the upper echelons of society in general, there was no lack of encouragement for this lighter type of music in the courts and capitals of Europe—nor indeed of rewards for composers who were prepared to meet the demand for it. Typical of the works produced are Haydn's twelve Divertimenti for harpsichord, two violins, and bass, written in the early 1760s when he was in the service of Count Morzin, the simple string parts of which were doubtless designed specifically to provide enjoyment for his aristocratic employer and various of his friends.[2]

Most widely cultivated of the early keyboard genres were the so-called accompanied sonatas, in which, following French models established originally in 1734 with two renowned sets of *Pièces de Clavecin en sonates avec accompagnement de violon* by Cassanéa de Mondonville, a solo harpsichord is accompanied by a violin in a simple supporting role, and sometimes also by a cello to strengthen the bass.[3] Important as early precursors of the classical violin sonata and piano trio, compositions of this type, despite—or perhaps because of—their dilettante character, were much admired, and continued to be cultivated at least until the first decades of the nineteenth century. Works for larger ensembles, with as many as three or four accompanying strings, being thus prototypes of the mature piano quartet and quintet, were produced with increasing frequency from the 1760s onwards, often by composers of distinction, such as the Mannheimers—Filtz, Holzbauer, and Richter;[4] the Viennese—Wagenseil, Vanhal, and Mann; and Guiseppe Cambini from Leghorn, whose light and melodious keyboard quartets enjoyed much popularity in Paris during the 1770s.[5]

musical compositions, one must . . . bear in mind the sort of amateurs a piece is written for, and whether the composer has not had to adjust to their abilities and taste. The composer of the present sonatas clearly wrote them for amateurs whose hands are not yet practised enough for great difficulties, but who nevertheless enjoy good, expressive melodies. And in this respect they are excellently composed.'

   [2] See H. C. Robbins Landon and David Wynn Jones, *Haydn, his Life and Music* (London, 1988), 70.
   [3] See William S. Newman, 'Concerning the Accompanied Clavier Sonata', *Musical Quarterly*, 33, 327. Also E. Reeser, *De Klaviersonate met Vioolbegleiting in het parjische Musikleven ten Tijde van Mozart* (Rotterdam, 1939), 43.
   [4] See R. Fuhrmann, *Mannheimer Klavier-Kammermusik* (Marburg, 1963).
   [5] D. L. Trimpert, *Die Quatuors Concertants von Guiseppe Cambini* (*Mainzer Studien zur Musikwissenschaft*, 1) (Tutzing, 1967). A detailed study of Cambini's string quartets, which also lists, and provides information about, his five keyboard quartets.

During this period, the string complement for keyboard quartets was normally two violins and a cello, and for quintets, the same with the addition of a double bass. The chief departure from this was the occasional substitution of a flute or oboe for one of the violins. Violas were used only rather rarely, but when present, provided significant pointers to future scoring patterns. The normally dominant role of the keyboard was to some extent diminished by the involvement of larger accompanying forces, since the ability of three or more strings to provide full harmony and perform independently encouraged the use of alternating tutti and solo sections, and thus created an important link with the contemporary concerto. Moreover, in some cases, concertante contributions of importance were allotted to instruments in the ensemble other than the harpsichord, so as to provide extra variety. But it was not until the last two decades of the century, and above all in the keyboard chamber works of Mozart, that a truly equitable distribution of material between the instruments began finally to be achieved.

Among the finest examples of the keyboard quartet at its earliest stage of development are four works by Johann Schobert, a native of Silesia who came to Paris in 1760 as harpsichordist to the Prince de Conti, and remained there until his untimely death (from 'mushroom' poisoning) in 1767. The leading figure in a coterie of expatriate German musicians, including J. G. Eckard, L. Honauer, and H. F. Raupach, he won popular favour not only with his numerous accompanied sonatas for harpsichord and violin, but also with several works for larger ensembles, including keyboard trios, quartets, and concertos.[6] Though little remembered nowadays, he was particularly admired in his time for the vigour and seriousness of his music, characteristics which made a powerful and lasting impression on the young Mozart, who met him in Paris during the autumn and winter of 1763–4. Of his four quartets, three—described as 'Sonates en quatuor pour le clavecin, avec accompagnement de deux violon [sic] et Basse ad libitum'—were published in 1767 by Vendome of Paris as his Op. 7 Nos. 1 in E flat, 2 in F minor, and 3 in G minor, and were subsequently brought to London by Charles Burney (so he claimed) in 1770, where they were reissued by Robert Bremner. The fourth

---

[6] H. Riemann (ed.), *Johann Schobert, Ausgewählte Werke (Denkmäler deutscher Tonkunst*, Leipzig 1909; repr. 1958; 39).

work, also in E flat, appeared (probably at about the same time) as the first item in his Op. 14, the remainder of which comprises five typical accompanied sonatas, with a supporting part for violin only. Each of the quartets has three movements, the first a sonata-form Allegro and the second and third either a minuet with a fast finale or a slow movement with a minuet finale. All three movements are cast in a simple binary form with repeats marked for each half and a recapitulation introduced at approximately the midpoint of the second half, observing a graceful formal pattern in common use at the period. The risk of inflexibility which such symmetrical structures invite is skilfully minimized by Schobert through phrase extensions and the frequent postponement of perfect cadences. And by adopting a quasi-orchestral style of keyboard writing he achieves an unusually wide range of expression, particularly in his minor-key movements. A notable example is the second movement of Op. 14 No. 1, an Andante in C minor, the title of which, 'Polonoise' (*sic*), no doubt reflects some nationalist influence absorbed by the composer from his native region near the Polish border. Majestic in style, with full chordal writing systematically doubled by the strings, it conveys an impression of power which points forward, however distantly, towards late Haydn or even early Beethoven.[7] Also very striking in this quartet is the sharing of material—principal theme and harmony—between the first and last movements, by which an unusually early example of 'cyclic' theme transference is achieved (see Ex. 1).

Some four or five years later, there were published in London, as his Op. 1, Six Quintets by Tommaso Giordani, which have been justifiably claimed (by Nicholas Temperley in a recent modern edition of three of them) as 'the first examples of what would later be called the piano quintet'.[8] Giordani, who was born in Naples

---

[7] It is noteworthy that, where simple doubling is involved, the relatively slight tone of the harpsichord or fortepiano is easily overpowered by the rich sonority of the three stringed instruments, even when, as in the first movement of Op. 14 No. 1, their parts are marked 'con sordino'. Thus the keyboard's assertion of its individuality is restricted to isolated unaccompanied sections, or to those in which it has passage-work pitched well above the strings. And, by a curious paradox, it is largely the 'ad libitum' strings, when present, which create the impressive overall tone-colour.

[8] N. Temperley (ed.), *Tommaso Giordani, Three Quintets for Keyboard and Strings* (*Recent Researches in the Music of the Classical Era*, 25) (Madison, New York, 1987).

Ex. 1. J. Schobert, Op. 14 No. 1
(a) 1st movement
(b) 3rd movement

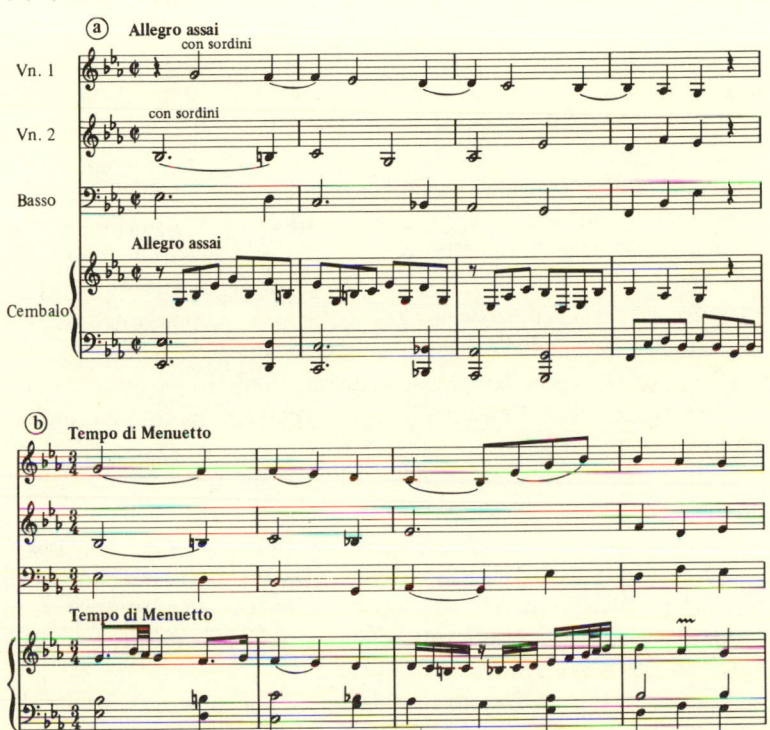

in about 1733, was one of a number of Italian musicians who lived and worked in London during the second half of the eighteenth century, including Felice Giardini, Pietro Guglielmi, and Gabriele Piozzi, all of whom were active in chamber composition. His quintets, each in three movements—fast, slow, fast—and frequently with a minuet-style finale, were not the first of their kind to appear; already in 1767 Giardini had issued, through Welcker of London, six similar works for harpsichord, two violins, cello, and bass. But they were almost certainly the earliest to combine the keyboard with the string complement of two violins, viola, and cello which was eventually to become standard. It is not, however, solely by their scoring that the Giordani quintets command attention. Altogether new for the

period is the way in which their principal material is shared ˌ
between the instruments, with a consistent limitation on the
normal tendency of the keyboard to dominate. A good example is
provided by his A major Quintet, the third in the set. This begins
with an extended tutti section of a distinctly orchestral character,
during which each of the strings, starting with the first violin, is
granted a share of the principal themes, with the viola and cello
fulfilling particularly important solo roles. The keyboard at first
provides only continuo support, and surprisingly does not
function as a soloist until the dominant key area is reached in bar
43, where it contributes ornamental features to a somewhat rudimentary second subject group. In the process an interesting compromise is achieved between concerto and accompanied sonata
structures. The concerto style, though plainly evident in the
opening tutti, stops short of including a double exposition or
consistent ritornello repeats; while the sonata style, though implied
by the central role of the keyboard, is constantly modified by
the lively contributions provided by other instruments in the
ensemble.

Similar features are apparent in two chamber works of Viennese
origin, both entitled 'Concertino', which date from the third
quarter of the eighteenth century: one, by Josef Anton Steffan, in
G major, for flute, violin, cello, and harpsichord; and the other, by
Leopold Hofmann, in A major, for the same combination, but
with an additional part for string bass.[9] Both works adopt the
customary three-movement pattern, and both have short tutti
passages at the start of each movement, out of which the keyboard
emerges as a concerto-style soloist, with the strings and flute
providing subsidiary, though by no means unadventurous, roles.
Noteworthy, in Steffan's quartet, is the fine writing in the slow
movement, an Adagio in G minor, in which thematic ideas are
passed gracefully between the keyboard and its supporting melody
instruments (see Ex. 2). Also related in style are six quintets 'for
organ or harpsichord and string quartet', dated 1776, by Antonio
Soler, a pupil of Domenico Scarlatti, who was *maestro de capilla*
of the Jeronymite monastery at El Escorial, near Madrid.[10] Typical

---

[9] M. Fillion (ed.), *Early Viennese Chamber Music with Obbligato Keyboard*, pt.
2 (*Recent Researches in the Music of the Classical Era*, 33) (Madison, New York,
1989), 12 and 44.
[10] R. Gerhard (ed.), Antonio de Soler, *Six Quintets* (Barcelona, 1933).

Ex. 2. J. A. Steffan, Concertino, slow movement

of his approach is the opening of his F major Quintet, the second
in the set, where a tutti for the strings alone proceeds for thirty-
two bars to a full close in the tonic. Then, in a manner suggestive
of a second exposition, the keyboard instrument enters unaccompanied with a reprise of the first five bars, and with the strings
supporting or vying with its solo contributions in true concerto
style, leads on through various modulatory adventures (including
a surprising move to E minor) to the dominant. Clearly reflecting
the influence of his teacher, the keyboard writing is brilliantly
effective, and adapted equally to the alternative instruments
specified.

Individual movements of larger proportions are to be found in a
set of works by J. C. Bach, which were issued by the London
publisher, J. C. Luther, in 1785, three years after the composer's

death, under the somewhat puzzling title: 'Three favourite
Quartetts and | One Quintett for the Harpsichord, Flute |
Hautbois, Tenor and Violoncello, | By the late John Christian
Bach, Esq.', with the express marking, in parentheses, '(Never
before printed)'.[11] The title is puzzling partly because the collection actually comprises a Quartet in G for keyboard and strings,
two Quintets, in D and F, in which the keyboard is joined, respectively, by flute, oboe, violin, and cello, and oboe, violin, viola,
and cello, and a Sextet in C (sometimes misattributed to J. C.
Friedrich Bach) for keyboard, oboe, violin, and cello, plus two
horns; and partly because two of the works, the quartet and the
sextet, had in fact been printed previously, in 1783, by Johann
André of Offenbach-am-Main. Appended to the collection, and
certainly not previously printed, was Luther's own arrangement of
all four works 'for the Harpsichord or Piano Forte, with a single
accompanyment for a Violin', a curious reversion to the favourite
accompanied sonata genre, expressly made 'in order to render this
capital Work as useful as possible'.

Together with his piano trios, these works are Bach's major
contribution to the keyboard-dominated chamber repertoire. Not
surprisingly, in view of his commitment to orchestral genres, all of
them show some degree of concerto influence. The first movements of the quartet and the two quintets, for example, each begin
with a mock orchestral tutti, in which the keyboard supplies
continuo harmony from a figured bass; and when the keyboard
solos eventually occur they are often left unaccompanied or, in
concerto style, with only the lightest of string support. A more
continuous keyboard part is evident in the sextet, possibly because
of its richer, more orchestral, scoring with horns; but the writing,
in which arpeggio and broken-chord patterns predominate, contributes more to sonority within the ensemble than to thematic
contrast. On the other hand, in the finale of the F major Quintet, a
'Minuet en rondeau', the keyboard functions as an obbligato
soloist only during a thirty-bar episode in the minor which
precedes the final return of the rondo theme.

The two published versions of Bach's G major Quartet, the
most forward-looking work in the collection, reveal some minor

[11] See Introduction to E. Warburton (ed.), *The Collected Works of Johann
Christian Bach*, 41, 'Music for Five and Six Instruments' (New York and London,
1986), viii–ix.

differences in scoring.[12] In the André print of 1783, the setting (presumably in accordance with the composer's original intention) is for a string complement of a violin and two cellos; while in Luther's 'Three favourite Quartetts' issue the first cello part is adapted for a 'viola obbligato', with necessary adjustments to suit the latter instrument's different compass. In the original version both cellos have independent roles, and not infrequently combine in parallel thirds or sixths to contribute inner sonority of much warmth. Moreover, the bass to the whole ensemble is provided at least as frequently by the keyboardist's left hand as by the second cello, and the latter, as a result, gains unusual freedom of movement within the texture.

The composer's handling of sonata form is well demonstrated by the first movement, a substantial piece of writing constantly characterized by energetic triplet patterns. Noteworthy are its extended second subject group, in which a succession of themes provide for pointed imitative exchanges between keyboard and strings, and its strong, expansive development section which, despite a limited key scheme, makes effective use of harmonies based on circles of fifths, and contains some of the most elegant scoring in the work (see Ex. 3). The only other movement, a rondo finale, begins with a principal theme of extraordinary naïvety for keyboard alone, the squareness of which is redeemed solely by a sudden string intervention, via a V–VI interrupted cadence, at bar 16, a harmonic and scoring strategy which is preserved exactly in each subsequent rondo return. The first of the intervening episodes provides for elaborate passage-work for all three strings, with the keyboard confined to a simple accompaniment, while the second gives particular prominence to the two cellos in a type of free variation of the rondo theme in the minor mode. Somewhat unusually, a sizeable coda is appended to the movement, in which Bach exploits most effectively a vividly operatic style with rattling demisemiquavers in the keyboard part.

Despite the publisher Luther's uncompromising description 'for the Harpsichord', the overall style of the quartet, the historical evidence, and specifically the rapid succession of *piano*, *cresc.*, and *forte* markings in bars 132–5 of the finale leave no room

---

[12] E. Warburton (ed.), *Works of J. C. Bach*, 40, 'Music for Four Instruments', 1.

Ex. 3. J. C. Bach, Quartet in G, 1st movement

for doubt that the keyboard instrument intended by the composer was the fortepiano. Luther's title seems, indeed, unusually restrictive for the period. Even as early as 1766, London publishers were already using the more comprehensive phrase 'Harpsichord or Forte Piano' for collections of sonatas or chamber works, the alternative instrument envisaged being no doubt the Zumpe square piano, then recently introduced to the capital. Among the sets of works published in that year, and similarly described, were Christian Bach's Op. 5 Sonatas of April/May, some of which, as Richard Maunder has shown in a recent study, contain crescendo markings, rapid dynamic contrasts, and a singing melodic style, indicative of the composer's leaning towards the newer instrument.[13] By the early

[13] R. Maunder, 'J. C. Bach and the Early Piano in London', *Journal of the Royal Musical Association*, 116, pt. 2 (1991), 201.

1770s grand pianos by the Dutch maker Americus Backers, substantial instruments with bichord actions similar to the somewhat later Broadwoods, were coming into normal concert use in London, particularly for concertos and works for large chamber ensembles. And throughout the whole ensuing period until Bach's death in 1782, newspaper advertisements provide repeated evidence of his preference for the piano in the performance of concertos and sonatas.

A choice of keyboard instruments, evidence of a lingering tradition, is also indicated in the original titles of both of Mozart's piano quartets. For the earlier of the two, K. 478 in G minor, first published by Hoffmeister in December 1785, the title reads 'Quatuor pour le Clavecin ou Forte Piano, Violon, Tallie [a misprint for Taille = viola] et Basse'; and for the second, K. 493 in E flat, Artaria's print of 1787 bears the inscription 'Quartetto per il clavicembalo o Forte Piano con l'accompagnamento d'un violino, viola e violoncello'. The whole style of the music, however, clearly precludes the harpsichord as a realistic option. The instrument which the composer had in mind was the 'Viennese' fortepiano of the period—probably a Stein, Walter, or Rosenberger—the bright, distinctive tone and mechanical responsiveness of which provided then, and still provides, for these works the best means of achieving clarity of texture and an effective balance with the strings. At the same time, while acknowledging the superiority in the context of the instruments of the day, it is worth observing that the fullness evident in much of Mozart's keyboard writing (a fullness little shared by earlier fortepiano music) is such as to make the modern piano—nowadays, of course, the most normal performance medium—a perfectly acceptable alternative.

According to the Danish music historian, Georg Nissen, who married Mozart's widow, Constanze, in 1809, the composer originally entered into an agreement with Hoffmeister to produce a series of three piano quartets; but the first of these, K. 478, according to his account, found so little favour with the public that a cancellation of the contract for two further works was mutually agreed between composer and publisher.[14] In the changed circumstances, therefore, it was Artaria who accepted the second work, K. 493, eventually publishing it in July, 1787. However, an

[14] G. N. von Nissen, *Biographie W. A. Mozarts* (Leipzig, 1828), 633.

unexplained mystery still surrounds the event, since the E flat
Quartet appears to have been completed by early June, 1786,
before the cancellation of the contract, and its violin part, surprisingly enough, to have been already engraved by Hoffmeister.[15]
Various reasons have been advanced for the resistance which the
sales of K. 478 are said to have encountered: that the piano
quartet was too new and unfamiliar a genre; that the music's
depth of expression and complexity of thought greatly exceeded
the limits of popular taste; and that the work provided too many
technical difficulties for the amateurs who were likely to be its
readiest purchasers.[16] These 'reasons', of course, though cogent
enough for a publisher in search of a profit, form a substantial
basis for the high regard which K. 478, and its companion quartet,
have enjoyed ever since; and it is hard to believe that Hoffmeister,
a composer himself of some distinction, did not at once recognize
the extraordinary merits of the G minor work. His decision to
cancel the agreement, with all the damaging consequences it was
likely to cause to his reputation in the long run, must have been
implemented only for the most pressing of financial reasons.

Two entrenched ideas about the E flat Quartet merit some
consideration. The first is that it was to some extent modelled on
the E flat 'Quatuor' (Op. 7 No. 1) by Schobert, referred to above.
It would be pleasant to suppose that Mozart had felt an urge to
link his composition with one he had first encountered in his
childhood, particularly since the earlier work can reasonably be
regarded as one of the foundations of the entire genre. However,
parallels between the two compositions, which are confined to the
openings of their first movements, are quite slight and may well be
coincidental. In addition to having a shared principal key, both
works start quietly (Mozart's string parts being marked, in a
contemporary hand, 'sotto voce') with long-held string chords in

[15] See Introduction to *Neue Mozart Ausgabe*, Serie viii, Werkgruppe 22/1,
(Kassel, 1957).
[16] The unfamiliarity of the serious Mozart style, and the degree of concentration
necessary for the performance of works in this category, was remarked upon by a
critic in *Journal des Luxus und der Moden* (Weimar, 1788). 'Such compositions',
he declared, should be performed 'by four talented musicians who have properly
studied them, in a room where not even the suspension of each note escapes the
ear, and in the presence of some three or four attentive people.' From M. S.
Morrow, 'Concert Life in Vienna, 1700–1800', University of Indiana dissertation,
1984, p. 22.

support of quaver movement on the piano, in the right hand in Schobert and the left hand in Mozart. In bar 3, where Mozart touches on the subdominant, Schobert proceeds to a C minor seventh chord; and in bar 4 where Mozart provides a falling dominant seventh arpeggio on the violin, Schobert, in his sixth bar, has a similar descent for the piano right hand. But thereafter, the two compositions proceed quite independently.

The second commonly held view is that, because of the adverse criticisms of its predecessor, Mozart tried to make the E flat Quartet more accessible to amateurs, a doubtful enough theory since, as we have seen earlier, the later work was almost certainly completed before the contract with Hoffmeister was cancelled. Nevertheless, while there is no reason to regard the second work as any less characteristic than the first, it certainly differs from it in mood, its E flat major key providing for a more lyrical form of expression than the severe G minor of its companion. Also, its texture is more open, more ventilated by rests, and provides larger solo roles for individual instruments, with fewer passages of contrapuntal imitation. But the idea that Mozart deliberately courted popularity by adopting a simpler style for the second work will hardly bear serious scrutiny. It was, after all, his frequent practice, when composing a group of works for a particular medium—such as his six 'Haydn' Quartets and his last three symphonies—to set them in contrasted keys, one of them often a minor key, and with a varied expressive content and compositional style to match.

The two quartets differ, however, not only in expression, but also in important structural details. In the first movement of K. 478, for example, the strongly etched opening motif (together with the answering phrases it engenders) dominates the entire first subject group up to bar 50. Its characteristic descending intervals of a fourth and a minor second gradually evolve, by enlargement or inversion, to new melodic shapes which, when modified by changes of harmony, mode, and dynamics, and set in imitation, provide what is, even within this relatively small area of the exposition, a highly concentrated form of development. Particularly striking in the last of these transformations, from bar 45, is the way the principal theme, with its downward leap extended to an octave, is presented in close imitation between the pianist's left and right hands against a graceful new countertheme, shared contrapuntally between violin and viola (see Ex. 4). The parallel

Ex. 4. Mozart, Piano Quartet in G minor, K. 478, 1st movement

section in the E flat work is only half as long and more settled in character, with elegant scale passages on the piano, lightly accompanied by the strings, as its principal feature. At bar 28, however, at the start of the second subject group, a striking two-bar phrase is introduced, comparable in weight to the G minor Quartet's opening motif; and this, detached from its melodic continuation, provides the material on which virtually the whole of the ensuing development section is based. In contrast, the development of K. 478 ignores almost entirely the work's opening idea, since it has already been exhaustively treated, and focuses instead on a wholly new theme, introduced initially in bar 104 on the piano. Thus, in the two movements, two quite different approaches to the conventional processes of exposition and development are explored.

In each of the first movements the second subject group comprises two principal themes, together with a separate cadential figure. In K. 478 the first of these gently ruffles the expressive surface of the music with asymmetric sforzando accents, by which two and a half bars of 4/4 time could well sound like two bars of 5/4, were it not for Mozart's carefully prescribed phrasing marks. In the recapitulation the theme recurs, characteristically, in the minor mode, and enriched by a new melodic surface in the violin part, and an additional sforzando. In the E flat quartet, after the vivid two-bar motif at the start of the second group, lyrical themes of distinctive character are presented, mainly by the violin alone with a simple piano accompaniment; but, again characteristically, new elements are introduced in the recapitulation, including a surprising initial lead to the dominant for the beginning of the second group, before a sudden switch restores the 'correct', home key, and a beautiful expansion for the strings alone (from bar 200) before the return of the second theme of the group, begun this time by the viola. However, despite some inequalities in their component parts, the two movements share not only the same number of bars (251), but also a similar grandeur of structure, the latter only fully realized when the repeats marked for both halves of their binary sonata schemes are observed.

The slow movements, though entirely equal in melodic beauty and technical finesse, show similar contrasts in structure. Both are in sonata form, with fully-fledged second subject groups, but have strikingly different internal proportions. In the G minor work, by the use of larger melodic phrases and more extensive repeated sections, Mozart provides an exposition which is nearly twice as long as that in the second quartet; as a result, he is able to dispense with a formal development and proceed after a link of only four bars to the recapitulation. In the second work, however, the more epigrammatic style provides space for a development section of considerable length, which includes a delightful snatch of 'canon three in one' for the strings, over a dominant pedal, as part of the approach to the reprise of the first theme. Furthermore, in the E flat work, at the end of the movement, where in K. 478 the recapitulation simply recalls, punctually, the closing bars of the exposition, there is room for further enlargement in the form of a fifteen-bar coda, by which the weight provided by the lengthy development section is gracefully counterbalanced. Both halves (excluding the coda) are marked to be repeated in K. 493, in contrast to the earlier work where the slow movement has no repeats.

Greater overall similarity is evident in the two finales, each of which follows an expansive sonata-rondo structure, made slightly irregular by a side-step of the normal second return of the main theme at the point of recapitulation. In the earlier work this results in an immediate recurrence of the first episode, and in the later one in an equivalent return of the second subject in the tonic key. This type of compression, found also in Mozart's mature piano trios of 1788, results partly in a general tightening of the musical argument, and partly in an increase in the climactic effect of the final coda. Charming and delightfully witty is the effect achieved in the G minor Quartet, where snatches of the rondo theme are woven into an elaborate preparation for its long-awaited second return, only for the expectations thus aroused to be finally cheated.

The choice of the major mode for the finale of K. 478 is unusual. Mozart's normal practice in his relatively few large-scale works in minor keys is to retain the original mode to the very end. The only other notable exception is the G minor String Quintet, K. 516, of 1787, where a special, somewhat enigmatic, twist is given to its major key finale by prefacing it with a sombre introduction in the minor. No such problematic aura is imparted to the piano quartet finale, the bright, carefree character of which may well have been designed (if, sadly, with little success) to enlarge its appeal to the amateur players of the day. The prodigality of Mozart's invention is everywhere apparent in the two finales: in K. 478, at bar 60, for example, where he 'borrows' a theme, no doubt unconsciously, from a quintet by J. C. Bach (his Op. 11 No. 6) and bends it precisely to his compositional purpose at that point; and at bars 341–2, where he enriches the coda by a dramatic use of a V–VIb interrupted cadence, recalling the procedure used with similarly telling effect in the first movement of his G major Piano Concerto, K. 453. Also very fine, in the E flat Quartet (at bar 85 and again at bar 293), is the manner in which, following a pause on a diminished seventh by the piano, he shifts the prevailing tonality, in the succeeding passage for strings alone, a tone lower in pitch (to A flat major in the first instance and D flat in the second) with an impressive, if momentary, increase in the gravity of expression (see Ex. 5).

For Mozart's immediate successors, the ideal balance between style, structure, and content which he had achieved in his chamber works with piano is likely to have provided a formidable discouragement to further progress along strictly classical lines.[17] Most nearly comparable to the Mozart quartets are Boccherini's two sets of six Piano Quintets, Op. 56 and Op. 57, written for what was to become eventually the standard ensemble of piano and string quartet. Completed in 1797 and 1799, they were

[17] H. Keller, 'Mozart—the Revolutionary Chamber Musician', *Musical Times*, 122 (1981), 465–8.

Ex. 5. Mozart, Piano Quartet in E flat, K. 493, finale

published, respectively, in 1800 and 1820, the first set with a
dedication to Friedrich Wilhelm II of Prussia and the second 'à la
Nation Française'. Avoiding the temptations of the concerto or
continuo-accompanied styles, the composer maintains an effective
balance between piano and strings, and, despite an excessive
leaning towards short repetitive phrases, achieves with these works
a significant landmark in the early development of the genre. The
general tendency, however, of the next generation of composers,
many of whom were virtuoso pianists, was to use the piano
quartet, sometimes enlarged to a quintet by the addition of a
double bass, as a vehicle for the display of their chosen instrument,
and of their own skills as performers, without over-much concern
for the deeper subtleties of the sonata style.

It is interesting to notice, however, that in 1785, some months *before* Mozart completed the first of his quartets, a set of three Piano Quartets, in E flat, D, and C, were composed by the fourteen-year-old Beethoven, no doubt under the critical eye of his teacher at the time, Christian Gottlob Neefe. Understandably, the works are very immature, though still remarkable for so young a composer. Reflecting the known interests of Neefe, they show to some extent the influence of the later chamber music of C. P. E. Bach, for example his accompanied sonatas (for keyboard, violin, and cello), Wq. 89–91, of 1775–77.[18] However, in the E flat quartet, the first and best of the set, a more specific influence is that of Mozart. The unusual form of the first movement—a lengthy Adagio assai in the tonic major, linked to an Allegro con spirito in the tonic minor—and the variation structure of the separate second movement point directly to Mozart's G major Violin Sonata, K. 379, of 1781, as a model; and any remaining doubts are dispelled by the close similarity between the opening Adagio themes of the two works. The individual variations of Beethoven's final movement provide solo roles for each of the instruments in turn—piano. violin, viola (with complex writing in demisemiquavers), and cello for the first four variations followed by two further ones in which the piano predominates—the manner of which the composer was again to adopt, very successfully, for the slow movement of his C minor Piano Trio, Op. 1 No. 3. No doubt discouraged by his teacher from attempting to publish the quartets, the young composer subsequently 'borrowed' parts of them for incorporation in other works, notably the 'Adagio con espressione' of the C major Quartet for the slow movement of his F minor Piano Sonata, Op. 2 No. 1. Eventually, however, they were rescued by Artaria, and issued posthumously in 1832, as a valuable relict of the composer's earliest years.

The precise part played by Emanuel Bach's chamber music in the formation of the young Beethoven's style is difficult to assess;[19]

---

[18] R. Oppel, 'Über Beziehungen Beethovens zu Mozart und zu Ph. E. Bach', *Zeitschrift für Musikwissenschaft*, 5 (1922/3), 30.

[19] A further influence of importance is likely to have been provided by the widely acclaimed flute quartets of Josef Anton Bauer (1725–1808), with which the young Beethoven became acquainted at Bonn during the 1780s. Published in Paris between 1770 and 1776, in three sets of five compositions each (Opp. 1–5), these works are scored for flute, violin, cello, and keyboard and reveal an advanced early classical style, in some cases with four-movement structures.

but the older composer's general contribution to the chamber repertoire, and particularly to the development of the piano quartet, during the last quarter of the century should not be overlooked.[20] Of special significance are the three keyboard quartets, in A minor, D major, and G major (Wq. 93–95), which he produced at Hamburg in 1788, the last year of his life. Scored for flute, viola, [cello], and fortepiano, these remained undiscovered after the composer's death until 1929, when autographs of the second and third quartets and a contemporary copy of the first were unearthed by Ernst Fritz Schmid, who subsequently published modern editions of them.[21] In the original scores a part for cello is not provided; but string support for the bass line is clearly intended, not least because, in the list of contents of his estate (which he himself compiled) the composer describes the quartets as written 'for keyboard, flute, viola and bass'. Each of the works is in three movements, of which the outer ones are normally in sonata form (the Andantino first movement of the A minor work, Wq. 93, exceptionally, follows a ritornello pattern), while the central slow movements, cast in the composer's typically emotional style, with drooping melodic figures, frequent appoggiaturas, and chromatic chord progressions, are freely ternary in structure. Apart from the opening movement of Wq. 93, the outer Allegros are entirely late-classical in manner, the finales, in particular, approaching closely to Haydn's mature style. Noteworthy, in the first movement of the D major work, is the rhetorical, decidedly Beethovenian, move to the flat submediant at the point of recapitulation, and the elegant use of an augmented sixth to restore the basic tonality (see Ex. 6).

Whether or not Beethoven knew of these last flowerings of the genius of Emanuel Bach is uncertain. But during the late 1780s and early 1790s it was in any case increasingly to Mozart, whom he had first met in Vienna in 1786, and who had prophesied a great future for him, and to Haydn, whose pupil he became from 1792 to 1794, that he turned as his principal models. Furthermore, at that period, he came significantly into contact with the work of Emanuel Aloys Förster, a considerable pioneer in the field of large-

[20] See E. F. Schmid, *Carl Philipp Emanuel Bach und seine Kammermusik* (Kassel, Bärenreiter, 1931).
[21] E. F. Schmid (ed.), C. P. E. Bach, Three Quartets, Wq. 93–5, Nagels Musik-Archiv 222/3/4 (Kassel/London, 1952).

Ex. 6. C. P. E. Bach, Quartet in D, Wq. 94, 1st movement

ensemble chamber works with piano.[22] A Silesian by birth, Förster had settled in Vienna in 1780, after service in the Prussian army, and it was there, in the early 1790s, that he gained the friendship and admiration of Beethoven, who called him his 'alter Meister'. He, too, was originally much influenced by C. P. E. Bach, but after 1780 began to cultivate the high classical style of Haydn and Mozart. His distinctive contribution to the chamber repertoire of the time included six Piano Quartets, Opp. 8, 10, and 11, and a Sextet, Op. 9, for piano, flute, bassoon, violin, viola, and cello, published in 1796.

It was probably during a visit he paid to Berlin in 1798 that Beethoven's most daring attempt to emulate Mozart was made, with his Quintet for piano and four winds—oboe, clarinet, horn, and bassoon—modelled precisely, with the same key, scoring, and structure (including the slow introduction, but not the elaborate cadenza in the finale) on the older composer's masterpiece, the E flat Quintet, K. 452, of 1784.[23] The attempt was 'daring' because of the rarity of compositions for such an ensemble, which made a direct comparison between the two works inevitable—a com-

---

[22] See R. M. Longyear, 'Förster', in *New Grove Dictionary of Music and Musicians* (London, 1980), 6, p. 717.

[23] After his Quintet's first performance at a Lenten Concert in the Burgtheater, Vienna, in April 1784, Mozart wrote to his father, in understandable excitement, 'I myself consider it to be the best work I have ever composed.' Letter of 10 April, 1784, in Emily Anderson (ed.), *The Letters of Mozart and his Family* (London, 1966), 2, p. 873.

parison which, in the event, has consistently, and certainly not unfairly, rated Beethoven's quintet less highly than Mozart's.[24] The latter's practice, especially during his first two movements, is to provide short, often two-bar, themes, ideally suited to the formation of sequences and counterstatements, and by parcelling them out to the different instruments in turn, to create a wonderfully kaleidoscopic pattern of tone-colours. Beethoven, on the other hand, writes longer, less easily divisible themes, and frequently allocates them in full to the piano alone, with the winds remaining silent until granted a restatement. He also places greater emphasis both on the purely harmonic function of the wind instruments as an ensemble, and on their roles (found chiefly in the slow movement) as individual soloists in extended passages involving a single tone-colour. Closely though he adhered to the structural pattern of his model, Beethoven in fact achieved a quite different kind of work; one, certainly, less varied and less subtle than Mozart's (as, by similar comparisons, quite a number of his earlier compositions may be regarded), but larger in framework, with a broader tonal scheme, and with many pointers towards the dramatic forms of expression he was later to exploit so intensively.[25]

At the time of the quintet's composition, Beethoven also provided a transcription of it for piano quartet—with violin, viola, and cello. The wind origins of the work are apparent in the octave and unison passages of the slow introduction and to some extent in the 6/8 'hunting' style of the rondo finale; but in general the transfer to the new medium is highly successful. The composer's preference for a quartet rather than a quintet texture for his arrangement reflects, no doubt, the greater popularity of the piano quartet in Vienna at the time; but it must have resulted also from his realization that a simple allocation of the original horn part to a stringed instrument was bound to be unsatisfactory. In order

[24] See D. F. Tovey, *Essays in Musical Analysis: Chamber Music* (London, 1944), 106, for a comparison of the Mozart and Beethoven Wind and Piano Quintets.

[25] In later years the Mozart and Beethoven Quintets provided models for numerous further contributions to the form (sometimes with varied scoring) by composers as widely distributed in date and style as Spohr, Berwald, Magnard, Florent Schmitt, Holst, Lennox Berkeley, and most notably, Francis Poulenc, whose charming *Sextuor* (1932–39) for piano, flute, oboe, clarinet, bassoon, and horn, richly deserves the wide popularity it has gained.

to solve this problem, and at the same time secure a balanced
distribution of interest, his rescoring often involves octave transpositions, up and down. A good example occurs in bar 52 of the
first movement where the viola takes the original clarinet line an
octave lower, the cello the bassoon part at pitch, and the violin
the horn part an octave higher. Only very rarely is any single
instrument required to do dull duty with long-held horn pedal
notes, an isolated example being the viola part in bars 169–80 of
the first movement. Elsewhere, significant changes involve the
creation of new string support for the piano part towards the end
of most of its longer solos, the provision of new string detail to fill
the extended breathing spaces previously necessary for the wind
players, and, in the case of the lengthier wind solos (such as those
in the slow movement for oboe and bassoon, transferred in bars
17–28 to violin and cello, and for horn, transferred in bars
57–63 and 68–73 to the viola) the addition of graceful ornamen-
tation to enhance the general character of the string writing (see
Ex. 7). The piano part alone remains unchanged from the original
version; and it is only on some of the rare occasions when the
piano is silent (such as bars 226–32 of the finale) that the strings
are expected to use double-stoppings in order to reproduce the
original four-part writing of the wind version.

As in all his mature explorations of relatively novel genres,

Ex. 7.
(a) Beethoven, Quintet for Piano and Wind Instruments, Op. 16, slow
movement
(b) Beethoven, Piano Quartet, Op. 16, slow movement

Mozart's scoring, in both the quartets and the quintet, is a miracle of precision, its consistent inventiveness resulting largely from the richness of his basic compositional technique. Elements of his approach can be seen if we compare scoring details in the exposition of the first movement of K. 452 with those at the corresponding points in the recapitulation. One example is provided by the second subject which, after its initial presentation on the oboe at bar 46, returns with entirely different sonority, on the horn at bar 100; and another by the complete reversal of the wind and piano roles when the cadence theme, originally at bar 61, reappears at bar 115. Even more striking, however, is the treatment accorded to the imitative passage involving ascending scales in demisemiquavers, which occurs initially at bar 57 of the exposition. At its first appearance, in a section comprising two-and-a-half bars, five scale patterns are allotted in turn to the clarinet, oboe, piano right hand, piano left hand, and bassoon; only the natural horn, with its restricted note-range, is forced in the context to remain silent. But when the passage returns in the tonic at bar 111, a further half-bar is skilfully inserted, so that an extra scale can be provided for the E flat horn, one which ranges easily upwards from B♭ over the best part of its compass (see Ex. 8). In the process not only is a form of 'generous compensation' provided for the instrument previously neglected, but also through the expansion involved, the closing paragraph of the movement is given additional grandeur in a small but highly effective manner. A similar variety of scoring is to be found in Beethoven's quintet, but of a more inflexible kind, prompted it would appear less by the sort of joyous creativity so evident in Mozart's work than by the changes in texture which the contrasts of key between the main sections of a movement almost inevitably entail.

During the next thirty years or so the piano quartet and quintet became, with some notable exceptions, the concern of minor chamber composers. Working under the shadow of Beethoven, but probably less overawed by his example than later generations who, with the advantage of a longer perspective, were able to comprehend more fully the magnitude of his achievement, these lesser figures gained widespread recognition for the colour and vitality of their music. Newly developed resources of Romantic melody and harmony, coupled with rapid advances in the tone-quality, compass, and mechanical efficiency of pianos, led to the

Ex. 8. Mozart, Quintet for Piano and Wind Instruments, K. 452, first movement

creation of an important new sub-species of chamber composition, one whose ancestry is most directly traceable, because of its focus upon a predominant keyboard part, to the accompanied sonata tradition of former times. In the process, however, the sonata structures were often less richly organized than formerly, and equality of instrumental partnership, one of the most hallowed of chamber criteria during the period of Viennese Classicism, was frequently sacrificed to the dominance over his colleagues of a single virtuoso performer.

2

The Early Romantics

PROMINENT among the first contributors to the new keyboard ensemble repertoire were the Czech pianist-composer, Jan Ladislav Dussek, and his royal patron and sometime pupil, Prince Louis Ferdinand of Prussia, a nephew of Frederick the Great. At the time of their first meeting, at Magdeburg in 1803, Dussek had already completed (probably in London in 1799) his Piano Quintet in F minor, a three-movement work comprising a sonata allegro, a slow movement in ternary form, and a rondo finale. The role of the strings—violin, viola, and cello, with an optional part for double bass[1]—is largely accompanimental, though the violin is granted some melodic passages and there are a few short sections for the string ensemble alone, such as the simple opening idea of the slow movement. The piano, on the other hand, has a vivid concertante part, covering a range of nearly five and a half octaves, which was clearly designed to exploit the power and extended compass of the latest instruments of the period.

No doubt it was Dussek's example in this work which prompted Louis Ferdinand, a soldier by profession, but also an accomplished pianist, to compose so intensively for keyboard and strings. His output, between 1803 and his untimely death, at the Battle of Saalfeld, in October 1806, includes a piano quintet, two piano quartets, and three piano trios, together with separate variation sets for piano quartet.[2] Essentially the work of an amateur, though a very skilled one, his compositions suffer from insufficiently varied textures, a tendency to repeat rather than develop, longwindedness, and, in his earliest attempts in particular, trite melodic ideas. But there is also much to admire in his confident management of

---

[1] In the few places where the double bass is independent of the other strings, its notes are already present in the piano part. However, though non-essential in that respect, the important ballast it provides to the ensemble, to offset the high keyboard writing, cannot be lightly sacrificed.

[2] H. Kretschmar (ed.), *Prinz Louis Ferdinand: Musikalische Werke* (Leipzig, 1910).

large-scale forms, his deployment of bold harmonies and unusual modulations, and his finely shaped piano writing with its emphasis as much on the singing qualities of the pianos of the time as on their capacity for brilliant display.[3] Described by Schumann as 'der Romantiker der klassischen Zeit', he provided, with his clear resolve to restrain mechanical virtuosity in favour of higher musical aims, an example, of substance and individuality, which was to prove attractive to many later composers, among them Weber, Hummel, Mendelssohn, Spohr and, eventually, Schumann himself.[4]

Louis Ferdinand's Op. 1, a Piano Quintet in C minor, published in Paris in 1803, is unusual for its period, partly in being scored for what was to become the standard string ensemble of two violins, viola, and cello, and partly as one of the earliest works of its type, in the new, proto-Romantic style, to involve a four-movement structure (presumably following the example of Beethoven's Op. 1 Piano Trios of 1795), with a minuet and trio, placed second. The strings, though generally subservient to the piano, are granted occasional melodic contributions, particularly for the restatement of second subjects; and although the cello enjoys less independence than the others, some compensation is provided for it in the slow movement where it features as soloist in the first of an elegant set of variations.

The finest of his chamber compositions, however, is his F minor Piano Quartet, Op. 6, a work which displays added dignity in its melodic ideas and an unusually subtle management of tonality. Typically ingenious in the first movement is the point of recapitulation, where, following a series of startling modulatory shifts, the main theme returns in B minor, the most distant of keys from the original tonic, only to slip smoothly back home, via a diminished seventh, four bars later (see Ex. 9). The finely focused second movement (entitled 'Menuetto', but a scherzo in all but name) creates, with syncopations and climbing sequences over a chro-

[3] Beethoven, who dedicated his Third Piano Concerto to the Prince, was well impressed by his musical abilities: 'his playing', he declared (according to an account by Ries), 'was not that of a King or Prince, but that of a thoroughly good pianoforte player'. Cited in A. W. Thayer, *The Life of Ludwig van Beethoven*, ed. H. E. Krehbiel (London, repr. 1960) i, 196–7.

[4] See B. H. McMurtry, 'The Music of Prince Louis Ferdinand', Univ. of Illinois diss., 1972.

Ex. 9. Louis Ferdinand, Piano Quartet in F minor, Op. 6, 1st movement

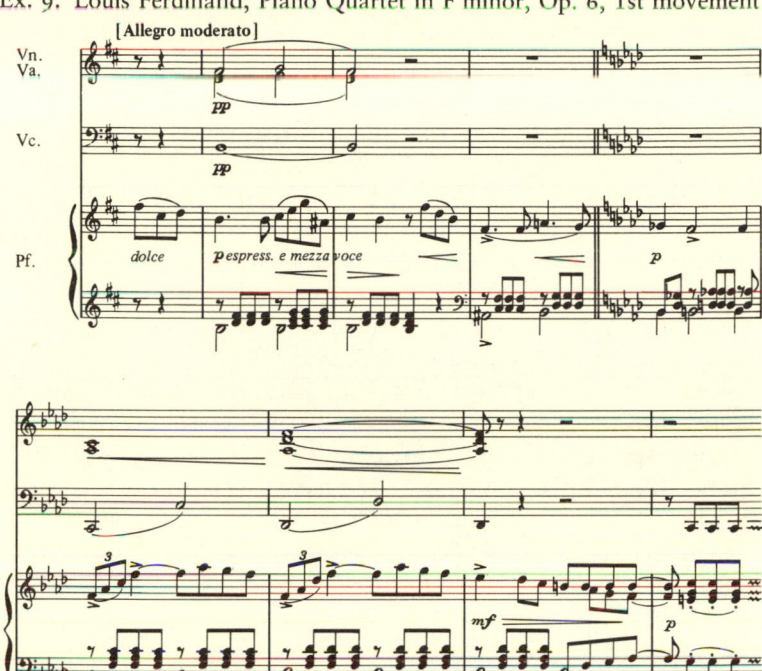

matic bass, a vividly colourful impression. But it is the third movement—'Adagio lento e amoroso'—that provides the focal point of the work. Modelled to some extent on the expansive slow movements found in various of Beethoven's early and middle period piano sonatas, such as Op. 22 in B flat, of 1800, it combines a glowing warmth of expression with a precise control of structure, disrupted only by an extended, somewhat superfluous, solo piano cadenza before the final return of the principal theme.

Most immediate among Louis Ferdinand's successors was Carl Maria von Weber, whose small but by no means insignificant contribution to the growing repertoire includes an elegantly designed Piano Quartet in B flat, which was published as his Op. 6. Originating as an Adagio in E flat for piano and strings, composed at Karlsruhe in 1806, the year of Louis Ferdinand's death, it grew into a full-length work some three years later at Stuttgart, by the addition of a sonata first movement, a minuet and trio (placed third), and a brilliant finale. The piano part is characteristically showy, but less obtrusively so than in many other chamber works of the period; and the strings are granted many idiomatic contributions, both energetic and lyrical. Of particular interest is the finale, the sturdy construction of which supports ideas of much vitality. Its opening theme has two contrasted segments: a four-bar phrase by the violin alone, which is immediately repeated with harmony on the lower strings; and a vivid descending passage in anapaestic rhythms on the piano. At the climax of the movement the first of these segments (marked ⓐ in Ex. 10) returns as a strongly etched fugue subject, with successive entries by the violin, viola, cello, and piano right hand, and is eventually linked with the second segment (marked ⓑ in Ex. 10) in a simple but highly effective piece of double counterpoint. This is one of the earliest instances of a fugal climax in the finale of a chamber work for strings and piano, and may well have provided the inspiration behind Schumann's similar procedure in the last movement of his

Ex. 10. Weber, Piano Quartet in B flat, Op. 6, finale

great quintet of 1842—not to mention the many other distinguished examples which followed later.

During the intervening years before the appearance of the Schumann quintet, the most important large-ensemble chamber works with piano were Schubert's 'Trout' Quintet, of 1819, which was published posthumously (by Joseph Czerny, of Vienna) in 1829, and two compositions by Hummel: his Septet in D minor for piano, flute, oboe, horn, viola, cello, and double bass, Op. 74, published in 1816, together with a quintet version for piano, violin, viola, cello, and double bass, under the same opus number; and his Quintet in E flat, Op. 87, usually claimed to have been composed as early as 1802, but not published until nearly twenty years later. In view of various connections between these works, it will be appropriate to examine them here as a group, despite their somewhat widespread dates of composition and publication.

The circumstances surrounding the creation of the 'Trout' Quintet are set out in a letter, written many years after the event, in 1858, by Schubert's boyhood friend, Albert Stadler. In this he reveals that the quintet was specially commissioned by Sylvester Paumgartner, an amateur cellist and ardent chamber music enthusiast, who not only asked for a variations movement based on his favourite Schubert song, 'Die Forelle', but also stipulated that the work should be modelled, in scoring and construction, on a particular quintet by Hummel.[5] It has sometimes been assumed that the chosen Hummel work was his famous Piano Quintet in E flat, Op. 87; but since in his letter Stadler uses the words 'the quintet, *recte* septet, of Hummel' it is clear that he in fact meant the piano quintet version of his D minor Septet. Furthermore his description of the Hummel composition as 'then still a new work', helps to confirm the date of composition of the 'Trout' Quintet as 1819, the first occasion when Schubert is known to have spent the summer in the village of Steyr in Upper Austria, where Paumgartner lived. The letter also contains an interesting phrase, deleted by the writer, to the effect that he had himself prepared the manuscript parts of Schubert's work for its first performance at Steyr, the deletion being explained as an attempt to be perfectly truthful, since, by 1858, after such a long time-gap, the writer

---

[5] See A. Butzer and J. Neubacher (eds.), preface to Schubert, Piano Quintet in A major, D. 667 (Edition Eulenburg, No. 118, min. score).

could not be sure of the trustworthiness of his memory. Any doubts, however, have recently been dispelled by the discovery by Arnold Feil, editor of the relevant volume of the new complete edition of Schubert's works, of Stadler's handwritten parts at the monastery of St Florian in Upper Austria.[6]

It is difficult to recognize in the 'Trout' Quintet any specific details which might have been prompted by Hummel's work, beyond its scoring with double bass, for which there were in any case models by other composers, and the fact that both compositions contain a variations movement. Other common characteristics, which are part of the normal vocabulary of each composer, are a fondness for third-related keys, such as the flat mediant and flat submediant, a frequent exploitation of the highest registers of the piano, and an insistent use of rapid figuration, often in quaver triplets in Schubert, and in semiquaver, or even demisemiquaver, quadruplets in Hummel.

Hummel's Septet is one of his most varied and effective chamber works. In keeping with the fashion of the day, and of his own particular leanings, he provides a piano part of great brilliance which naturally tends to dominate the texture. But his use of three wind instruments—flute, oboe, and horn—far from giving the accompanying ensemble an orchestral character, contributes to a true chamber texture, patterned with distinctive threads of colour. By contrast, the piano quintet arrangement, though perfectly effective, is necessarily more monochrome, and thus rather less well adapted to the overall style of the music. In the first movement, an extended sonata structure, both the principal themes are cast in the march-like style often cultivated by the composer, and in the present case well suited to the large mixed ensemble. The energy of the first subject group tends, however, to become dissipated by an excess of full closes in the tonic—no less than six in the first thirty-four bars—before enharmonic changes to F sharp minor and back to D flat major lead to the second group in the relative major. Then, using a system commonly applied by the early Romantic composers we have been considering, and one which, from a classical viewpoint, tends to distort the sonata structure, Hummel continues his second group with a torrent of brilliant

---

[6] See A. Feil (ed.), preface to *Franz Schubert, Werke für Klavier und mehrere Instrumente* (*Neue Ausgabe sämtlicher Werke*, Serie vi, 7) (Kassel, 1975).

keyboard patterns, which is preserved to the end of the exposition. This ensures that, when the passage returns finally in the tonic, an excitingly virtuosic ending is achieved; and, more beneficially, that an effective backcloth is provided for the skilfully constructed development, with its series of swift modulations and lively sections of dialogue between the instruments.

The second movement (also in D minor, and quaintly described as 'Menuetto o Scherzo', despite being wholly un-dancelike, with its flashing arpeggios and heavily cross-accented chords) is notable for its somewhat irregular structure. Instead of proceeding to a full da capo repeat after his major-key Trio, the composer brings back only the last 41 bars of the Scherzo and follows them with a second appearance of the Trio; and then, delightfully and unexpectedly, simply ends with a 10-bar coda over static D major harmony. In its general style this movement sounds remarkably 'modern' for its period, anticipating the quicksilver type of writing cultivated particularly by Saint-Saëns, many years later. More orthodox in character, the variation movement in F major which ensues is based on a four-square theme of much charm, treated in a wholly classical manner with patterns of increasing elaboration applied to its basic harmonic structure, and with one contrasted variation in the minor. The first phrase of the original theme returns repeatedly at the end of the movement in a decorated form, much in the way that the song theme is recalled at the end of the corresponding movement in the 'Trout' Quintet, though the elaborate piano figuration which supports it is in marked contrast to the simple setting (drawn from the original Lied) which Schubert provides. In the powerful finale, the composer incorporates a fugato section as part of his first subject group, initially in D minor and subsequently, in the recapitulation, in B minor; and thus provides, with a type of 'thumbprint' found in several of his major works, such as the finale of his A minor Piano Concerto, Op. 85, a welcome touch of contrapuntal interest.

Hummel's only original piano quintet, his Op. 87 in E flat, again scored with a double bass instead of a second violin, has gained widespread popularity for the freshness of its ideas, and represents a major, if somewhat outlandish, contribution to the genre. Immediately striking is the composer's retention throughout the work of the same tonic, E flat, and his curious use of a major key signature (with accidentals applied as necessary) when all the movements, except the short slow movement, are actually in the minor mode. Very possibly he feared that a six-flat signature would discourage potential purchasers and for that reason may have considered altering his basic tonic. But it is clear that, whatever he did, his odd choice of subsidiary keys, particularly in the first movement—E flat minor for the first subject group and A major, initially, for the second—was certain to land him in notational difficulties. In the first movement, the necessary moment of enharmonic change occurs at bars 41–2, where a dominant seventh in G flat proceeds to a 5/3 chord of D (= E double flat) major, with a change of key signature from three flats to two sharps, and subsequently, through an augmented sixth on D♮, to C sharp major, as the dominant of F sharp, representing G flat, the mediant in the basic key (see Ex. 11). So far so good; but after a further fifteen bars in C sharp, a single bar leads to A major— only interpretable in the context as B double flat major—for the first of the two markedly operatic ideas which comprise the second group. During the last thirty bars balance is regained when F sharp major is confirmed as the principal subsidiary key area. The irregularity of this key and theme relationship inevitably arouses curiosity about the difficulties which seem bound to arise in the recapitulation; and here the composer's solution is even more remarkable than the original problem. After re-introducing the first subject, in the tonic minor, for only eighteen bars, he turns to the major mode for one of his characteristic fugato sections and follows it by an entirely new 'second' subject. No trace remains of either of the original second themes and, with the minor mode eventually restored, the music moves gracefully to a pianissimo ending. Whether representative of Romantic bravado or simple eccentricity, the whole scheme is carried through with such remarkable panache that it creates its own persuasive rationale as it proceeds. It would be interesting to know, however, whether the novel key and theme sequence was pre-planned, or whether it occurred, more or less by chance, during some process of improvised composition.

After a minuet and trio of orthodox structure, the slow movement starts with a grave introduction of eight bars, followed by an expressive theme for the piano, in a Chopinesque bel canto style, and a series of delicate keyboard *fioriture* over an extended dominant pedal which leads, 'attacca', into the finale. The idea of

Ex. 11. Hummel, Piano Quintet in E flat, Op. 87, first movement

abandoning such a movement after only 29 bars, and joining it directly to its successor, was not without several classical precedents; but Hummel may well have been working directly from a particular Beethoven model, such as his Piano Sonata in E flat, 'Quasi una Fantasia', Op. 27 No. 1, of 1801, in which a link of a very similar type occurs.

Like a number of his 'early Romantic' contemporaries, Hummel shows a marked preference for minor keys in his large-scale compositions, and not infrequently, as in the case in both the works we have been considering, retains the minor mode until the very end. One part of his aim was no doubt to achieve a particular expressive colouring; but another may well have been to find solutions to a number of taxing technical problems. The creation of impressive thematic ideas, for instance, may often have proved easier for him within an overall minor colouring, as may also variety of harmony, and the organization of key centres in relation to his total structural plan. It is interesting however to observe how little the leading composers of time, with their strong classical roots, appear to have been affected by the general trend. Beethoven, for example, in his piano sonatas composed after 1801 (a total of fifteen works from Op. 31 onwards), adopted basic minor keys in only four cases; while Schubert, in many of his last compositions, including the A major and B flat Piano Sonatas, D. 959 and D. 960, and the C major String Quintet, D. 956, all of 1828, gave repeated evidence of his capacity for profound expression in major keys.

Profundity of expression seems not, however, to have been Schubert's principal concern in the 'Trout' Quintet. By general consent, this five-movement composition is one of the lightest and most lyrical of his chamber works, a reflection, it is said, of a summer holiday spent in the company of the singer, Michael Vogl, in the beautiful countryside at Steyr. However, the generally relaxed mood of the work is as much the result of the composer's careful planning of his key centres, with its special emphasis on keys to the flat side of A major, as of his charming thematic material and colourful scoring. The subdominant (D major) fulfils a particularly important role: as the main key for the recapitulation in the first movement (paralleling in this respect the finale of A major Piano Sonata, D. 664, composed at Steyr during the same period); as the key of the Trio to the central Scherzo, with its delightful excursion into B flat major in its second half; as the key of the entire fourth movement, the 'Die Forelle' variations; and as the very unusual key for the second subject group in the finale. Also, a warmly contented mood is provided by the use of the flat submediant (F major) for the Andante second movement, a key relationship subtly hinted at from bar 11 of the 'introduction', at the beginning of the whole work, before the first subject group gets fully under way at bar 25 (the *real* start, as is confirmed by its return in bar 210 for the recapitulation). Also contributory to the openness and gentle simplicity of the work is the way in which whole sections are repeated, often unaltered apart from changed key centres. The process is explored with great imagination in the Andante where, initially, three sections are built up, each with their distinctive thematic ideas, in F major, F sharp minor, and D major, leading to a close in G major (the dominant of the dominant). Then, in a sudden move, A flat major is established for the repeat of the first section, followed, with precisely parallel relationships, by A minor for the second section, and F major for the third. However, since any further exact repetition would have led to an ending in B flat, an extra bar (104) is inserted, which passes through a G minor chord to the dominant of F major; and thereafter, from bar 105 (matching bar 44 of the opening) all the subsequent music falls a tone lower than before, and so the home tonic is finally restored. The apparent simplicity of Schubert's art at such moments as this conceals a wealth of intricate thought, carried through with consummate skill.

A somewhat similar system of repeats in the finale provides a curiously shaped, but nevertheless wholly satisfying, structure. In the course of a sonata-style movement, the end of the exposition is followed immediately by a recapitulation in the dominant (E major), without an intervening development section; and since the original second group was set in the subdominant, no further adjustment is needed to ensure a final close in the tonic. If in fact the exposition is repeated (as marked by Schubert), its three appearances, exact apart from the key displacement and various octave adjustments in the final one, produce a striking symmetry, curiously rondo-like in effect.

The famous variation movement from which the work takes its title is the first in Schubert's chamber music to be based on one of his own songs. Later examples are found in the D minor String Quartet, D. 810 (1824), on 'Der Tod und das Mädchen', and the Introduction and Variations for flute and piano, D. 802 (1824), on 'Trockne Blumen' from *Die schöne Müllerin*. In a well-judged sequence, the variations divide into those which are founded simply on the basic melody—the first three, in which the theme is allotted in turn to the piano in octaves, the viola, and the cello and double bass in octaves—and those which are based more on the structure, harmony, and phrasing of the theme—Nos. 4 and 5, which introduce, respectively, a change of mode (to the minor) and a change of key (to B flat), and in both cases, a move to F major at the double bar. Particularly attractive, in the massively scored fourth variation, are the imitative exchanges between piano and violin which provide delicate contrast at the start of the second half; and in the B flat variation, the graceful modulation in bars 120–4, a move from D flat major through its minor chord (treated as C sharp minor) to A major, by which both the home tonic and the basic theme—at last with its original leaping song accompaniment on the piano—are finally restored.

Because of some discrepancies between the first published edition of the quintet (that by Joseph Czerny of Vienna in May 1829) and the newly-discovered instrumental parts which Albert Stadler made for the first performance in Steyr, questions have arisen about the exact type of double bass which Schubert envisaged. The problem concerns the lowest notes provided in the two versions. In Czerny's edition the bottom notes given are D' and C'—for example in the octave-leaping passages in bars 49–52 and 97–9 of the Andante—indicating the need for a five-string violone with C' as its lowest string; whereas in Stadler's part these lowest notes are avoided, by the elimination of the downward octave leaps in the passages cited, and uncertainty is shown about the availability of a bottom E', suggesting that the instrument intended was probably a four- or five-stringed double bass with the so-called 'Viennese' tuning of the time: (F'), A', D', F♯, A. While no definite conclusion can be reached, all purely musical considerations, including a comparison of parallel passages in the work, suggest that, whatever may have been available to him for the Steyr performance, the composer's final preference may well have lain with the deeper, five-stringed violone.[7] No doubt the inclusion of a double bass in the scoring reflects more the wishes of Paumgartner, who was anxious to provide for the ensemble he had already enlisted to play Hummel, than any particular desire on Schubert's part to write for such a combination. But there is no evidence in the music that the composer found its presence in any way irksome. Indeed, the instrument's part not only provides

---

[7] The matter is discussed in some detail in A. Butzer and J. Neubacher, op. cit., (see note 5). It may be significant that, in the double bass part of Schubert's Octet, D. 803, of 1824, notes of deeper pitch than F' appear to be avoided, in one or two places, by octave transpositions—for example in bars 47–9 of the Menuetto and 12–17 of the Finale.

strength in the bass to offset the high piano writing, but also makes numerous significant contributions in terms of harmony and instrumental colour. Striking examples in the first movement's exposition include the pizzicato arpeggio patterns in bars 26–32, underpinning the strings-only section of the first subject, which create an immediate impression of both lightness and strength; the rising triplet passage in compound minor thirds with the cello, at bar 52, vigorously outlining a diminished seventh chord; and in the development, from bar 165, the audacious but, when delicately controlled, wholly effective solo entry in E flat, echoing the smooth melodic idea previously delivered pianissimo by the violin and piano in turn.

Both Schubert and Hummel contributed also to the piano quartet repertoire, the former with an Adagio and Rondo Concertante, D. 487, of 1816, a salon piece which involves an uncharacteristic amount of technical display for the pianist, and the latter with a Quartet in G major, of uncertain date, the two movements of which, an 'Andante cantabile' in G major and an 'Allegro con spirito' in D, may well be the only surviving parts of a full-length work, whether actual or only intended.

Altogether more significant is the contribution made by Mendelssohn, between his twelfth and sixteenth birthdays, with three piano quartets—No. 1 in C minor (1821), dedicated to Prince Antoine Radziwill, No. 2 in F minor (December 1823), dedicated to Carl Zelter, and No. 3 in B minor (January 1825), dedicated to Goethe—and a sextet in D major for piano, violin, two violas, cello, and double bass, composed during May 1824. The three quartets were each published within a year of completion as Opp. 1–3, but the sextet was held back, probably because of its unusual scoring, and appeared only posthumously, in 1868. What cannot fail to astonish in these boyhood works is the composer's sure technical command, his control of large structures, his inventiveness, and his depth of musical understanding. The speed with which he developed these abilities during his teenage years is attributable not only to his phenomenal innate talent, but also to the highly supportive nature of his family background in Berlin. Regularly, on alternate Sundays, musical 'parties' were held in the home, at which new compositions by both the young composer and his greatly gifted sister, Fanny, were performed. Often distinguished patrons and friends were present to provide discerning criticism, among them Professor Carl Zelter, director of the Berlin Singakademie, Ferdinand Hiller, composer and pianist, and Ludwig Berger, the principal piano teacher of the two children. Further important contributions to the moulding of his musical character came from his contact with Weber, whom he met in 1821 when the older composer was present in Berlin for a production of *Der Freischütz*, and from a visit with his father to Paris, in 1825, where he basked in the company of many leading composers and performers of the day, including Cherubini, Hummel, Onslow, Rode, Baillot, and Kreutzer.

Of the three quartets, the third, in B minor, is certainly the best, being full of significant ideas,[8] handled with confidence and originality, and surpassed in technical mastery only by the superb Octet for strings in E flat, Op. 20, completed later in the same year. A notably successful structural experiment occurs in the first movement, where the development section, marked 'Più Allegro', is dominated by a new theme (starting in C major, the flat supertonic), with a fragment of the original first subject repeatedly set against it as a special type of motto theme (marked (x) in Ex. 12). And at the end, where a parallel section, with the same 'new' theme, but uninterrupted this time by the motto, serves as an extended coda. Earlier, in the exposition, the motto provides pointed commentary in a similar way on the main theme of the second group. And in subsequent movements it re-appears in two significant contexts: as the basic shape underlying the opening theme of the Scherzo, and as an emphatic part of the last climax of the finale (see Ex. 12). The cyclic interconnections thus created are of a type which was relatively new at the time, and, according to contemporary reports, urged on the young composer by his piano teacher, Ludwig Berger. A similar system of transference occurs also in the Piano Sextet, where a substantial section of the D minor third movement (marked 'agitato', and strangely entitled 'Menuetto') is recalled, and further developed, towards the end of the finale, giving in the process added substance, and a totally unexpected minor-key ending (apart from the last three bars), to what is otherwise a somewhat superficial movement, excessively dominated by pianistic display.

---

[8] Perhaps over-full, as Cherubini seems to have suggested, when he remarked of the young composer in 1825, 'il dépense trop d'argent, il met trop d'étoffe à son habit', quoted in P. Radcliffe, *Mendelssohn*, 3rd edn. (London, 1990), 9.

Ex. 12. Mendelssohn, Piano Quartet in B minor, Op. 3
(a) First movement
(b) Third movement
(c) Fourth movement

The emphasis on minor keys, throughout the series of quartets, is very striking, particularly in the work of a boy composer who was reputedly of a carefree, mercurial disposition. In a manner reminiscent of Hummel, and reflecting like him a common practice of the time, each of the three quartets is sent on its way in a grimly serious and purposeful manner, with the minor mode not only present in all the outer movements and scherzos, but preserved in each case to the final bar. In the opening allegros, relief is provided by the song-like second themes, set invariably in the relative major and usually followed to the end of the exposition by a rush of major-mode pianistic display. But the chief source of contrast resides in the warm lyricism of the slow movements, each marked by its colourful key relationship to the original tonic: the sub-mediant (as commonly in Beethoven) in the C minor and F minor works, and the major subdominant in the last of the set. Particularly attractive is the sense of repose created by the Adagio of No. 2 in F minor with its warmly Romantic principal theme, its adventurous middle section, during which an enharmonic change moves the tonality gracefully to E major (= F flat major) and back, via A flat minor, and its mysterious closing bars, with strings alone, pianissimo and tremolando, supplying a shifting chord pattern over a tonic pedal.

Among the scherzo-type movements, those in the C minor and B minor works already give evidence of the delicate, fleet-footed writing which was later to become a hallmark of the Mendelssohn style. Charming contrast is achieved in the C minor Quartet between the brilliant moto perpetuo writing in leaping quavers of the scherzo and the smooth, song-like character of the middle section in the major tonic, scored literally as a trio, with the cello (carrying the melody) supported from below by viola and piano left hand. Even more masterfully inventive, however, is the Allegro molto of the Third Quartet, with its darting patterns of semi-quavers, vigorous descending string lines in the central B major section, and occasional judicious irregularities of phrasing. A notable stroke is the high entry of the violin with the 'trio' theme, set against the phrasing, 31 bars before the end, an effect which, at rehearsal, was said by the young composer to have caused the violinist, Baillot, 'to make a mistake several times' with the result that 'he got into a terrible rage with himself'.[9]

Although the piano dominates the scene, the strings are no mere accompanists, but continually provide idiomatic contributions, including at times initiating a movement as a solo ensemble before the piano enters. In the Sextet the presence of two violas in the scoring tends to drive the cello down to a somewhat unadventurous supporting role as the bass of the harmony, with the double bass simply strengthening it at the unison or lower octave. But in compensation, the use of the violas in harness often contributes a special degree of warmth to the string texture which contrasts most effectively with the rapid, high-pitched patterns of the piano part (see Ex. 13). Mendelssohn's choice of instruments in the Sextet may reflect the availability of particular group of

[9] J. Horton, *Mendelssohn Chamber Music*, BBC Music Guide (London, 1972), 17.

Ex. 13. Mendelssohn, Sextet (1824), first movement

players at the time of its composition, though an earlier example for the same combination exists in the Sextet, WoO 76, by Ferdinand Ries, composed *c*.1814. In other sextets of the period, however, the more usual string ensemble of two violins, viola, cello, and double bass is adopted, for example, in two compositions by Onslow (arrangements of his own wind and piano works) and one each by Glinka (his 'Gran sestetto originale in E flat'), and Ries (a different work, his Op. 100). Closest in style to Mendelssohn, however, is a Sextet in F sharp minor by Sterndale Bennett, which was written between July and December, 1835, when the composer was nineteen, and published later as his Op. 8. The two central movements, a scherzo and an Andante, are skilfully devised and contain music of colour and vitality, but the outer movements are impaired all too often by an excess of empty brilliance in the keyboard part.

A reaction against the virtuoso piano style in chamber music came eventually in the work of Robert Schumann. Although one of the most keyboard-orientated composers of the period, he was nevertheless constantly opposed to the idea of pianistic display for its own sake, both in his own compositions, and, as is evident from his writings, in the work of others. As a result his chamber textures lack some of the variety of scoring found in those of earlier composers, since the piano parts, often confined largely to the middle of the keyboard, tend to double the strings at pitch rather than oppose them with high bravura writing. But in compensation, particularly in the larger chamber ensembles, a strongly unified texture is achieved, one well able to benefit from his 'symphonic' attitude to theme distribution and development, and from his natural skill as a contrapuntist.

The word 'symphonic' is used advisedly, since there is reason to suppose that a quasi-orchestral mode of thought may have underlain much of Schumann's piano writing, for example in his thick textures, his emphasis on inner melodic lines, and his frequent use of successions of widespread chords. A possible clue to his thinking is provided by the score of his early Piano Quartet in C minor, a work in four movements—Allegro, Menuett, Adagio, and Finale—which was composed at Heidelberg between 1828 and 1830, but remained unpublished until recently.[10] Entries in the composer's diary refer to various stages in the work's completion, and to a 'try-out' with friends which took place in March 1829. But the dissatisfaction which he eventually felt with it in its original form surfaces in January 1830 with the comment: 'Nichts. Das Quartett wird zur Symphonie umgeschüstert' (Nothing for it.

[10] W. Boetticher and H. Redlich (eds.), Schumann, Piano Quartet in C minor (Wilhelmshaven, 1978).

The quartet will [have to] be cobbled together as a symphony).[11] In the surviving score, a number of orchestral scoring indications provide hints about the way his thoughts were turning, though nothing, of course, came of the idea. It was, incidentally, in this early piano quartet that Schumann also began to sense the beginnings of a new style in his music. In a much later diary reference (in Tagebuch VIII of 1846–50), he confided: 'I well remember one place among my compositions [of 1828], which seemed to me to be Romantic; where I had departed from the style of older music and taken on a new poetic spirit—it was the Trio of the Scherzo [actually Minuet] of a piano quartet.'[12]

It was not, however, until 1842, the year following the appearance of his earliest major orchestral scores—the First Symphony, the A minor *Fantasie* for piano and orchestra (later to become the first movement of his Piano Concerto), and the initial attempt at his D minor Symphony—that Schumann became fully committed to chamber composition. After a period of intensive study of the classical repertoire, shared with Clara, he produced in hardly more than nine months, and despite a break enforced by overwork, his three String Quartets, Op. 41, the Piano Quintet in E flat, Op. 44, the Piano Quartet in E flat, Op. 47, and the first of his piano trios, entitled *Fantasiestücke* and published later as Op. 88. The Piano Quintet appears to have been composed in the white heat of inspiration during a period of barely a month, between the end of September and late October. Interesting evidence of the urgency of its creation is provided by an early sketch of the work (dated on its front cover: 'vom 23–28 Sept. 42'), which is now preserved in the public library at Carpentras, France.[13] Obviously written in great haste, with missed accidentals and poor legibility, this gives, on a single stave, a broad outline of the complete composition, with many numbered but empty bars, and indica-

---

[11] See W. Boetticher, 'Das frühe Klavierquartett C-moll von Robert Schumann', *Die Musikforschung*, 31 (1978), 465.

[12] 'Sehr gut erinnere ich mich einer Stelle in einer meiner Kompositionen (1828), von der ich mir sagte, sie sei romantisch, wo ein von der alten Musik abweichender Geist sich mir eröffnete, ein neues poetisches Leben sich mir zu erschliessen schien (es war das Trio eines Scherzo eines Klavierquartettes).' Cited in W. Boetticher, *R. Schumann, Einführung in Personlicheit und Werk*, Phil. Diss. (Berlin, 1939), 354.

[13] See J. A. Westrup, 'The Sketch for Schumann's Piano Quintet, Op. 44', in H. Hüschen and D.-R. Moser (eds.), *Convivium Musicorum, Festschrift Wolfgang Boetticher zum sechzigsten Geburtstag* (Berlin, 1974), 367.

tions of harmony, counterpoint, and instrumentation provided only at focal points. Clearly it was the composer's aim to capture on paper with all possible speed the ideas which were burning so intensely in his mind.

Some points of particular interest emerge from the sketch. One is that the work was originally intended to have five movements (like Schubert's 'Trout' Quintet), the additional section being an Adagio in G minor, marked 'Scena', and placed third, between the March and the Scherzo of the finished composition. Only some 40 bars are included in the sketch, involving arpeggio figurations and the outline of a cello melody, after which the movement seems to have been abandoned as clearly unsuitable. A second point relates to the well-established account by Friedrich Niecks, based on evidence supplied by Theodor Kirchner, that, in one of the middle movements, a new 'second trio' was introduced by Schumann in place of the original one, on the recommendation of Mendelssohn who, after he had played the work 'famously at sight' at a private performance in 1842, declared the section to be 'wanting in liveliness'.[14] Unfortunately Niecks's account does not state unequivocally which of the movements contained the supposedly offending 'trio', and as a result two later interpretations have been proposed: that the reference is to the Scherzo (most obviously, since the expression 'second trio' is used) or alternatively, that it is to the March, with the second, agitato, episode in F minor, as the substituted section. However, as the sketch plainly shows, no replacement was in fact provided for either section, which remain in their final forms precisely as originally planned, apart from a halving of the note-values in the final version of the agitato passage in the March. If the suggestion attributed to Mendelssohn is in fact correct, it may with greater probability have referred to the *first* of the Scherzo's Trios, the canonic entries of which are supplied in the sketch but not the piano figuration, the addition of which certainly imparted 'greater liveliness' to it. Lastly, it is interesting to notice that the sketch contains no indication of the famous fugal combination, at the end of the finale, of the principal themes of the first and last movements, suggesting that this idea may have come as a last-minute inspiration after much of the work was already completed.

[14] See F. Niecks, *Robert Schumann: A Supplementary and Corrective Biography* (London, 1925), 221.

Underlying the array of compelling themes which characterize the Quintet, there is present a musical framework of much strength and subtlety. Overriding his normal inclination towards the epigrammatic and episodic, Schumann provides for his themes to grow organically in a simple but highly effective way. Thus one or other of the splendid leaping intervals of the opening theme—the minor seventh, minor sixth, and octave—are found at the head of successive paragraphs during the first 50 bars, and continue to provide interior detail not only during the lead into the second subject (on the cello in bars 52 and 54) but also, contracted to a perfect fifth, during the development section. At the same time excessive sectionalization is skilfully avoided by the use of overlapping phrases and the ingenious deployment of interrupted cadences, notably at various phrase-endings in the major supertonic during the second subject group, where the intervention of a major ninth chord on F disrupts the expected full close. Also, following a common classical practice, the composer provides a cogent ending to the exposition by bringing back his first theme in the dominant, and in the process eliminates any need for the customary show of keyboard virtuosity at this point. In contrast to the richly melodic style and varied instrumentation of the exposition, the development is dominated largely by the piano, using continuous figuration derived, by diminution, from notes 4 to 11 of the first subject. The keyboard writing is athletic and the support from the strings relatively meagre, but both are so closely bound to the principal motifs from the start of the movement that any sense of empty display is readily dispelled.

The two inner movements, both episodic, are organized symmetrically with contrasting sub-sections, or trios, set in different related keys. The March, in C minor, has the overall shape ABA'CA''B'A''' plus a short coda. The B section is in the tonic major, C ('agitato') in F minor, B' in F major (the subdominant), and A''' in F minor, initially, with a return to the tonic after 6 bars. An exceptional degree of integration is created not only by the recall, before the C section, of solemn descending scale passages, first heard preceding the start of the development in the first movement, but also by a hidden relationship between the themes of the agitato C section and the basic march section (see Ex. 14); and furthermore by the ingenious preservation throughout section A'' of the triplet patterns from section C, pitted against the march theme on the viola.

Ex. 14. Schumann, Piano Quintet in E flat, Op. 44, 2nd movement

The shape of the third movement, a favourite one of Schumann's, is of a scherzo with two trios, the first in G flat major and the second in A flat minor, plus a coda. Here, again, a connection with the first movement, even though a slender one, is introduced, as the calm descending fifths of the canonic theme in Trio 1 supply a shadowy reflection (in inversion) of the vivid leaping patterns at the opening of the whole work. In the second Trio contrast is provided not only by its minor mode colouring, but also by its substitution of continuous quadruplet semiquavers for the Scherzo's triplet patterns. The key signature is restricted to four flats, and successive modulations through F flat major and minor, C flat minor, and G flat minor commit the composer to some complex notation problems (reminiscent of those of Hummel), which involve, for convenience, much enharmonic change.

For the finale Schumann constructs a remarkable type of ritornello movement, in which the principal theme returns in a wide range of keys, a process which he also adopted, though less extensively, for the finale of his D minor Piano Trio, Op. 63. Starting in G minor (from its subdominant chord of C minor), and thus providing effective key variety from the E flat major of the Scherzo, the main idea recurs at spaced intervals in D minor, B minor, G sharp minor, D sharp (= E flat) minor—the nearest approach to the home tonic—B flat minor, and eventually returns to G minor; thereafter it features, at its original pitch, as a fugue subject, from bar 248, with 'answers' in D minor and C minor, and, in altered form, as the countersubject in a double fugue, based on an augmentation of the opening theme from the first movement. To offset the relative severity of this scheme, lyrical episodes are interpolated in a variety of major keys, based on two scalic, marching motifs, both of which start, like the 'ritornello' theme itself, on the half bar. The first of these, a rising pattern at bar 21, becomes, in diminution at bar 43, a true second subject, in G major, while the second, heard first on the viola in bar 51, features prominently in what passes for a development, from bar 95, and is eventually embroidered delightfully, at bar 115, with a new countertheme on the strings.

Theme transference between the movements, culminating in the reintroduction of the first subject of the first movement in the finale, is worked out with unusual thoroughness in the quintet. Possibly Schumann was prompted in this by the example of Mendelssohn's early B minor Piano Quartet, or his String Quartet in E flat, Op. 12, where the practice is similarly, if less insistently, explored. However, evidence that the procedure was being increasingly adopted by chamber composers of the period is provided by the first of César Franck's Piano Trios, Op. 1, of 1841, in which elements drawn from two motto themes in the first movement are incorporated in both the second and third movements;[15] and by the Piano Quintet in D minor, Op. 130, of 1845, by Louis Spohr, in which a descending pattern in semiquaver sextuplets, a prominent feature throughout the first movement, recurs most effectively in a new quaver triplet configuration as the principal idea of the lengthy trio section in the ensuing Scherzo.

Immediately on completion of the quintet, Schumann started work, again apparently with feverish haste, on his Piano Quartet, finishing it barely four weeks later, at the end of November, 1842. Somewhat surprising is his choice of E flat major for this work, written so soon after his quintet in the same key. With his clearly subjective approach to the moods and colours of particular keys, he might well have been expected to seek creative stimulus from a different tonality. However, despite their shared key centre, the two works are in fact markedly different in expression. Where the quintet is expansive, majestic, and lyrical, the quartet, apart from its slow movement, is energetic, intensely contrapuntal, and often somewhat abrupt.

In the opening slow introduction all three strings use double stoppings to achieve a chordal texture of unusual richness, with four- and even five-part harmony. Schumann is fond of double stoppings, but the exceptional degree to which they are used here

---

[15] See B. Smallman, *The Piano Trio: Its History, Technique, and Repertoire* (Oxford, 1990), 138.

invites speculation that the opening may have originated as a first idea for the piano quintet, or even that this later work may have been planned, initially, in quintet form. To begin the Allegro, three abrupt chords, derived from the introduction, lead through a crescendo to a held dominant seventh, and then immediately to the first subject, a single-line theme for the piano right hand alone. The unusual character of this opening suggests that there may have lurked in Schumann's memory, from his studies of the great Viennese repertoire, the opening of Beethoven's third 'Rasumovsky' String Quartet, with its similarly mysterious slow introduction, followed by a sudden leap into a solo line for the first violin in the ensuing Allegro. But any such relationship is soon discarded in Schumann's continuation, which, though lyrical at first, becomes progressively more peremptory in manner. At bar 64, for instance, following a full close in the tonic, the second subject group begins abruptly on the dominant of G minor, and on the second beat of the bar, producing a startling, though temporary, disruption of the harmonic rhythm. And later, at the end of the exposition, where the introduction returns in the tonic, as if in anticipation of a full repeat, a dominant seventh in E flat is quitted as an augmented sixth on B♭ which sweeps the music, again with extraordinary brusqueness, into D minor for the start of the development. The effect of these, and several other, dramatic changes is to produce an exhilarating, sharply profiled movement, the forward drive of which is greatly enhanced by the powerful contrapuntal imitations which characterize it, particularly during the second subject group. As so often with Schumann the piano dominates the scene and the texture is thickly woven, but there are moments also of gracious interplay between the instruments in the purest classical manner (see Ex. 15).

The dark Scherzo, a moto perpetuo in G minor, hints at the aura of fantasy found in various parts of the composer's *Kreisleriana*, Op. 16 (1838), and in his setting (from 1840) of Heine's humorous poem 'Es leuchtet meine Liebe' (also recognizable as the inspiration behind the Scherzo of his A minor String Quartet, Op. 41 No. 1). In the second half, following some vigorous canonic entries of the strings against the keyboard and vice versa, the piano is given the last word in a four-bar, arched phrase, the final eight notes of which provide virtually all the melodic material needed for the imitative first Trio which follows, still in the tonic

Ex. 15. Schumann, Piano Quartet in E flat, Op. 47, 1st movement

minor. The regularity of phrasing maintained in the Scherzo and its first Trio is loosened in the second Trio by means of some off-beat patterns typical of the composer. Chords placed on the third beat of each triple-time bar obscure all sense of the prevailing bar-rhythm for 16 bars, until, at letter F, normality is restored by the reintroduction of fragments of the basic scherzo theme.

Effective lyrical contrast is provided by the slow movement, set in B flat and featuring a principal cello theme of impressive eloquence. A middle section in the flat submediant has a hymnic simplicity, only partially disguised by some further 'limping' dis-locations of the bar-rhythm, which seem to betray the composer's almost neurotic fear of writing in what he regarded as an inflexible manner. Inflexibility, however, returns prominently enough in the reprise of the principal theme, now allocated to the viola, where the addition of a relentless pattern of semiquavers on the violin, though clearly decorative in intention, is too rigidly maintained to provide a wholly satisfactory accompaniment. To end the movement, brief anticipations of the main theme of the finale are spelt out by the upper strings, while the piano supplies largely superfluous doublings, and the cello, with its bottom string lowered a whole tone, an octave B♭ pedal bass. This is an ingenious piece of scoring, but not one likely to win much favour with the participating performer. It is difficult not to wonder whether it was part of a carefully considered plan, or simply an expedient forced on the composer by his original choice of key. In the event the need for the cellist to retune before the start of the finale cannot help but detract from the thoughtfully devised motivic link between the two movements.

The lengthy finale is constructed partly on fugal and partly on sonata lines. Its opening theme (shown in Ex. 16) comprises three

Ex. 16. Schumann, Piano Quartet in E flat, Op. 47, finale

separate segments (marked ⓐ, ⓑ and ⓒ), each of which, at later stages, makes an individual contribution to the fugal argument. Segment ⓒ appears first, as the opening phrase of the main fugue subject, the pattern of which is distantly related to that in the finale of Beethoven's 'Hammerklavier' Sonata; stated initially by the viola, it is answered at dominant pitch by the piano and subsequently, at tonic and subdominant levels by the violin and piano in turn. The cello, surprisingly (but perhaps to allow for some surreptitious adjustments to the pitch of the bottom string), takes no part in the fugal exposition. At later stages, from bar 73 for example, segment ⓑ features in a complex series of stretto entries, involving all four instruments, and segment ⓐ, the shortest of all, in overlapping chordal patterns, from bar 81. Finally, in a splendidly 'symphonic' coda, segment ⓐ is enlarged into a separate countertheme, starting on an upbeat, against which is set a still further extended version of ⓒ to bring the movement to an exciting finish. The sonata structure includes, after the development, a central episode in A flat, the interlinked themes of which, set in answering phrases, are progressively inverted, not only melodically but also freely in double counterpoint; and, following a method of expansion which Schumann also employs in his early piano sonatas, a repeat of the entire development section during the recapitulation, transposed up a fourth to terminate in the home key.

The two Schumann compositions, and particularly the Piano Quintet, are nowadays recognized as the culmination of virtually all previous explorations of the genres, and at the same time as the foundations on which numerous later composers were able to build. The Piano Quartet has never been accorded the same recognition as its predecessor, largely because its principal themes lack the immediate attractiveness of those in the Quintet. It is, however, in many ways a more powerful work and, with its wealth of contrapuntal writing, more cogently constructed. It is regrettable that even nowadays it appears only rather rarely in concert programmes. The particular favour enjoyed by the Quintet during the years immediately after its composition is evident from the many performances it received. The first occurred in November 1842, at the Schumann home with Clara as pianist and a quartet led by Ferdinand David; and this was followed by a second, also at a private house in Leipzig, barely a month later. It was on this second occasion, with Clara indisposed, that Mendelssohn took the piano part at short notice and is said to have offered advice on how the work might be improved (see p. 44). Public performances followed in the Leipzig Gewandhaus in January and February 1843, and subsequently, up to 1848, the work received repeated airings, each time with Clara as pianist, at St Petersburg, Berlin, Prague, Vienna, and, finally, in Leipzig again.[16] Least happy of these occasions was that held in Leipzig in March 1848, when a performance was arranged specially for a much heralded visit by Liszt, who was *en route* to Weimar. Not content with arriving some two hours late, and comparing Schumann's beloved

[16] See R. Taylor, *Robert Schumann: His Life and Work* (London, 1982), 231 and 252.

Mendelssohn unfavourably with Meyerbeer, the great virtuoso is said to have described the Quintet as 'somewhat too Leipzigish', an observation which, understandably, was not taken as a compliment.[17]

[17] See R. Taylor, op. cit., 264.

3
Cross-Currents

FROM the middle of the nineteenth century, for at least a hundred years, works for large keyboard ensembles began increasingly to occupy a central position in the chamber field. One reason for this was certainly the widespread success of Schumann's inspirational Piano Quintet, which, by establishing what was virtually a new genre, with a specific aura of Romanticism, created an immediate ideal for composers of varied backgrounds to attempt to emulate. Naturally it was those of Austro-German origin who took a leading role, providing a continuing line of descent, which was to survive unbroken at least until the time of Schoenberg and Hindemith. But in other parts of Europe also, after a somewhat tentative start, a significant flow of new works began, often finely crafted and of an engagingly varied character. Links with the central tradition were continually in evidence, not least because many of the composers involved received their basic musical training in Germany; but fresh approaches, frequently inflected by national or folk 'dialects', created cross-currents which ruffled, beneficially, the surface of the German 'mainstream', both absorbing strength from it and infusing new elements into it. Thus, to take the simplest of cases, the intellectual discipline gained by Dvořák through his immersion in German symphonic ideals was paralleled, obversely, by the rustic vigour imparted to various of Brahms's works through his predilection for folk music, especially that of Hungarian origin. The synthesis achieved in these and other instances led, naturally, to an increased degree of cosmopolitanism; but this was offset by the prominently nationalist features found in the work of several of the most independent-minded composers of the time—those particularly whose origins lay in countries most geographically distant from central Europe.

One notable example was the Swedish violinist and composer, Franz Berwald. Born in 1796, a year earlier than Schubert, he was at first largely self-taught as a composer; but in 1828 a scholarship enabled him to study in Berlin, where he met Carl Zelter and the nineteen-year-old Mendelssohn, and absorbed many of the essentials of the central European style. Subsequently he achieved considerable success in Vienna with his opera, *Estrella di Soria*, and with various orchestral pieces; but sadly, recognition in his home country largely eluded him. Nowadays he is remembered chiefly for the four symphonies he composed between 1842 and 1845, which reveal independence not only in their unusual structural features and strange turns of melody and harmony, but also in their resolute avoidance of the more subjective or rhetorical aspects of Romanticism.

It was not until 1849 that Berwald embarked seriously upon chamber composition, producing during the next ten years four piano trios, two piano quintets, and two string quartets.[1] The preponderance of works with piano is surprising in view of his early training as a violinist and lack of significant skills as a pianist; and it is undeniable that his most accomplished works are his quartets for strings alone. His keyboard trios and quintets are none the less full of interest for their stylistic traits, and certainly effective in performance. Their piano parts, despite being somewhat orchestral in character and often very demanding, are designed with sensitive keyboard poetry in mind rather than extravagant virtuoso display. As the composer trenchantly put it in the foreword to the second of his quintets: 'it would be very agreeable to me if every crowd of virtuosos, who play only with the fingers and not with the head and the heart, would kindly ignore my compositions'.[2]

The two piano quintets—issued by the Hamburg publisher, Schuberth, as 'Op. 5' in C minor and 'Op. 6' in A major, in July 1856 and September 1857, respectively—had curiously tangled origins. The C minor work, which was composed in 1853, is described in the autograph source as 'No. 2', apparently because it had been preceded by a composition of the same type in A major (composed c.1848–50), of which the only movements to survive

---

[1] I. Bengtsson and B. Hammar (eds.), *Franz Berwald, Sämtliche Werke, 13, Klavierquartette und Klavierquintette, Monumenta Musicae Svecicae* (Kassel, 1966).

[2] Ibid., preface, xv. 'Dagegen wäre es mir sehr angenehmn wenn jene Schaar von Virtuosen, die nur mit den Fingern, aber ohne Kopf und Herz spielen, meine Composition gefälligst ignoriren möchten.'

complete are an intertwined Larghetto and Scherzo. In the auto-graph of this earlier work, there remain of the first movement only the last 23 bars, the rest having been torn out and, presumably, destroyed. However, since these final bars are identical to those at the end of the first movement of 'Op. 6', it is more than likely that 'Op. 6' is a reworking of the earlier A major Quintet, with a new Scherzo and Andante replacing its discarded movements and a new Finale added. And if, as seems probable, the 'Op. 6' Quintet was completed before the C minor one, but held back for later publication, this would explain any inconsistency in the sequence of their opus numbers.[3]

Berwald's fondness for unorthodox structures is evident as much in the completed quintets as in the surviving movements of the discarded one. Not only does he interlink all the movements, but also, in several cases, interpolates one movement inside another. In the C minor Quintet, for example, he interrupts the opening movement, a stormy Allegro in C time, after only 34 bars, with a lengthy 'Scherzo' in the tonic major, a leisurely, somewhat quirky dance in operatic style, with an ornate piano part and much effective pizzicato writing for the strings (see Ex. 17). Subsequently the opening section returns, unchanged apart from a short link to the succeeding 'Adagio quasi Andante'. Even in his more con-ventional sonata movements, there is often an unusual disposition of material. For example, in the finale of the C minor work, after 96 bars of development, there is suddenly inserted an exact repeat of 20 bars from the second subject group of the exposition before the development is allowed to proceed. Such 'irregularities' appear not to have worried the reviewer with the initials C. P. (possibly the Danish composer, Carl Petersen) who, in a survey of Berwald's chamber works in the Hamburg *Neue Zeitschrift für Musik* of April 1859, declared the last movement of the C minor Quintet to be 'as satisfying a finale as . . . one can hardly find surpassed, even amongst the chamber music of our best masters'.[4]

The model for Berwald's structural innovations is most likely to have been the symphonic poems of Liszt, several of which, including *Les Préludes*, *Tasso*, and *Prometheus*, appeared in

---

[3] Ibid., preface, xv.

[4] Ibid., preface, xv. 'Einen so nach allen Seiten hin befriedigenden Schlußsatz, wie dieser ist, wird man im Bereich der Literatur für Kammermusik kaum von unseren besten Meistern übertroffen finden.'

Ex. 17. Berwald, Piano Quintet in C minor, Op. 5, Scherzo

1848–50, at about the time that the Swedish composer began his extended series of chamber works. The first, and apparently only, meeting between Berwald and Liszt took place in April 1857, when the former was in Germany on a business trip. And on that occasion, according to a letter he wrote some three months later, he was delighted when some of his music was performed by the great Hungarian pianist. 'I heard my C minor Quintet played by a truly noble master', he wrote, 'at sight, into the bargain: that *was* music! It was no longer a piano but a full orchestra!'[5] Sub-

---

[5] Ibid., preface, xv. 'Ich hörte einmal mein C molls Quintett von einem wirklich poetisch erhabenen Meister—noch dazu vom Blatte—spielen! das war Musik! Es war nicht mehr ein Piano, sondern ein ganzes Orchester!'

sequently, at the end of 1857, on the basis of their developing friendship, Berwald dedicated his A major Quintet, 'Op. 6', to Liszt, and was rewarded, in April of the following year, by a letter from the Hungarian praising the new work in glowing terms. 'This quintet', he wrote, 'breathes . . . an atmosphere more rarified, more intellectually stimulating ['tonique'], than that which impels many good productions of its sort . . . the treatment is ingenious, skilful, and supple, the developments and transitions masterfully arranged, the style noble and of a harmonious originality.'[6] No doubt Liszt was attracted particularly by the unorthodox features of Berwald's work. More equivocal was the criticism which appeared in the Hamburg *Neue Zeitschrift für Musik* of April 1859: 'To a greater extent than in the previous work', wrote the reviewer, 'he pays homage in a different direction' [presumably a sly reference to Liszt]. 'No longer . . . is there the specific national–poetic character which made the earlier work so attractive. By comparison the new concept has gained extra life and fire, but it reveals a certain emptiness and lack of freedom. Nevertheless, the work has beautiful features in a grand style, and is in many respects superior to much of modern times'.[7]

It is hardly surprising, in view of the unconventional nature of so many of his ideas, that Berwald should have had frequently to defend himself from hostile criticism. Already, in 1821, one of his earliest chamber works, a Quartet in E flat for piano, clarinet, horn, and bassoon, composed in 1819 (the same year as Schubert's 'Trout' Quintet), became the subject of controversy between the composer and the critic of the Stockholm *Argus*. In a defence of his methods, published in the *Allmänna Journalen* of 31 March 1821, Berwald frankly acknowledged the experimental nature of

---

[6] Ibid., preface, xv. 'Ce Quintetto . . . respire . . . une atmosphère plus raréfiée, plus intellectuellement tonique, que celle dans laquelle se meuvent les bonnes productions en ce genre . . . La facture y est ingenieuse, habile et souple; les développemens et les incidens maîtrement ordonnés; Le style noble et d'une harmonieuse originalité.'

[7] Ibid., preface, xvi. 'Es huldigt das Werk theilweise einer anderen Richtung, als die vorigen, und zwar der neuesten. Dieses Werk lange nicht mehr jenen eigenthümlichen poetisch–nationalen Charakter hat, welche uns die früheren Werke so anziehend machte. Dagegen haben die Gedanken ein anderes Leben und Feuer bekommen, sind aber trotzdem, den früheren gegenüber, von einer gewissen Leere nicht ganz frei zu sprechen . . . Dessenungeachtet ist das Werk von grossartigen schönen Zügen und hebt sich in vieler Hinsicht über viele der Neuzeit.' *Neue Zeitschrift für Musik*, 50 (1859), No. 19, pp. 205–6.

his work, remarking particularly on his 'new treatment of instrumentation'.[8] The Quartet, a three-movement work in a style more
suggestive of Weber than of any other leading contemporary,
has in fact few very startling features, beyond a boldly operatic
manner of writing for the wind instruments, and a fondness for
tremolando effects for the keyboard.

In Russia progress in chamber composition was quite slight
before the last third of the century, when there appeared the
mature string quartets of Borodin and Tchaikovsky, together with
piano trios by Arensky and Tchaikovsky, and a quintet for
wind and piano by Rimsky-Korsakov. The only work to add
significantly to our particular sphere of interest is the early Piano
Quintet in C minor by Borodin, which was completed in July
1862, at Viareggio, where the composer spent the summer in
the company of his fiancée, the pianist Ekaterina Sergeyevna
Protopopova, who was recuperating after treatment for tuberculosis.[9] During that year Borodin not only completed his initial
scientific studies, and undertook important research at Pisa, but
also, in December, was appointed to a readership in chemistry
at the St Petersburg Academy of Medicine. The summertime composition of the Quintet represented, therefore, something of a
relaxation from his pressing professional concerns at the time,
though the work lacks, on that count, nothing in seriousness of
approach or care for technical detail.

The Quintet has three movements, an Andante, followed by a
Scherzo and Finale, which pursue a scheme of progressive tonality
unusual for the period. Although not interlinked, each of the first
two movements ends in the key of its successor, providing the plan
I: C minor to A minor; II: A minor to C major; III: C minor to C
major. The warmly lyrical opening Andante makes no pretence of
being a fully worked-out sonata movement. Two themes of
folk orientation, the first with prominent modal flat leading-notes
and frequent changes of time-signature, are simply juxtaposed in
appropriate keys—C minor and E flat in the exposition and F
minor and C major in recapitulation—with a modicum of intervening development. The ensuing Scherzo is a lively folk-dance in

[8] Ibid., preface, xiv.
[9] G. Abraham, 'The Chamber Music Works', in Borodin: The Composer and
his Music (London, 1929), 119.

duple time, rather in the manner of a Gopak or Trepak, with forte
chords occuring explosively on the final quaver beat of both the
main theme and its succeeding phrases. An equally lively second
theme, in the modally related key of G major, leads to C major for
a trio section, once again of folk character, which provides a
charmingly relaxed air of contrast. It is noteworthy that, in addition to their obvious modal colouring, many of the themes,
including some of those in the finale, have note-patterns in common (often outlining a 'gapped' descending scale), which, without
involving actual theme transference, contribute much to the overall unity of the work (see Ex. 18).

Ex. 18. Borodin, Piano Quintet in C minor
(a) 1st movement
(b) 1st movement
(c) 2nd movement
(d) 3rd movement

At about the time that Borodin, the 'amateur' composer, finished
his first truly successful chamber composition, his Czech younger
contemporary, Dvořák, who had completed his professional
studies at the Prague Organ School, where he had acquired a deep
insight into the classical repertoire, began the formation of a
personal chamber style, with a series of works, including a string

quintet and six string quartets, composed between 1861 and 1874. It was not, however, until the first half of 1875 that he produced his earliest fully successful works for piano and strings, the Piano Trio in B flat, Op. 21, and the Piano Quartet in D, Op. 23, both of which show marked progress towards a truly individual style. The Piano Quartet is in three movements (unusually for Dvořák it has no dance movement), the first of which is notable for its balanced classical structure and flexible themes which, being based largely on arpeggios, combine naturally and easily for developmental purposes. There are reminders of Schubert in the imaginative scoring and in some of the modulatory procedures, but the general musical language is unmistakably personal, with its motivic repetitions, clear-cut rhythmic patterns, and delicately varied harmony. Notable features of the first movement include the juxtaposition of the tonic, D major, and the major submediant, B major, in the first statement of the opening theme, and the exotic chromatic slides, first heard at bar 83, which add frequent touches of colour as the musical argument unfolds.

The central slow movement, a theme and variations, provides an outstanding early example of a form which Dvořák was later to cultivate with particular success—in his Piano Variations in A flat, Op. 36, Symphonic Variations, Op. 78, and String Sextet in A, Op. 48. The theme, in B minor and of regular binary structure, forms the basis of five variations and a coda, in which melodic reshapings and contrasts of scoring, often involving song-like dialogues between individual instruments, play a principal role. Key variety comes strikingly to the fore after the third variation, where a nine-bar linking passage shifts the tonality from the dominant of C major to E flat for the ensuing variation. Altogether delightful at this point is the subtlety of the piano's responses to the initial idea in E flat, on the strings. Set in C flat minor, but notated enharmonically in B minor, these repeatedly recall the movement's original key, but create for it an entirely new tonal orientation (see Ex. 19). At the end of the variation, with fine judgement, the composer clouds over his 'false' B minor with a diminished seventh and proceeds through their dominant sevenths to C major and G major, so that the original tonic can return entirely refreshed for the final variation. The last movement starts with a charming cello melody which, unhappily, becomes 'trapped' in a number of short-scale repetitions from which the composer

Ex. 19. Dvořák, Piano Quartet in D, Op. 23, 2nd movement

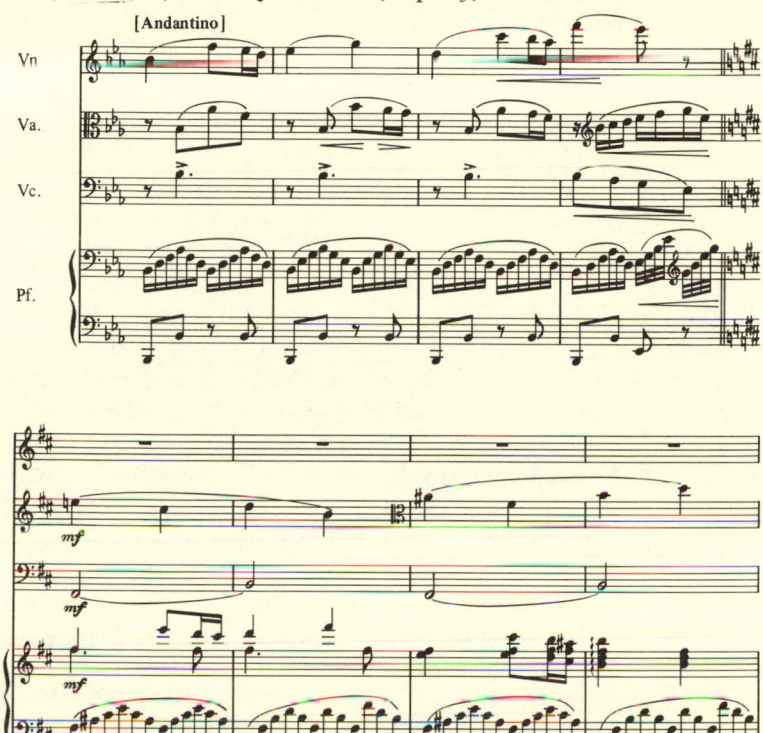

appears to have found difficulty in escaping. His solution—a series of rising sequences, based on bars 3 and 4, which lead to a new section at a faster tempo—is somewhat disruptive in effect, and subsequently the movement as a whole becomes excessively sectional. However the generous flow of the composer's melodic ideas proves as irresistible as ever, and the final transformation of the second subject into a dancing pattern in 6/8 time provides a brilliant, if somewhat abrupt, conclusion.

The speed with which Dvořák developed in his early chamber works becomes evident when one compares the polished D major Piano Quartet with his first attempt at a piano quintet, a three-movement work in A major which he wrote some three years earlier, in 1872. Although laid out on a broad scale, and full of imaginative ideas and colourful touches of scoring, this earlier composition is wildly discursive in style and shows little discipline, either in the handling of tonality or in the shaping of its structure. During the decade preceding its composition, Dvořák, as a viola-player in the Prague Theatre Orchestra, had become immersed in German Romantic music, of Schumann and, most particularly, of Wagner (who had actually conducted the orchestra in a concert in February 1863), and it may well be that the weaknesses in the Quintet reflect his difficulty in assimilating the many new impressions which had crowded in upon him. A thoroughgoing revision of the work, and a subsequent performance of it in Prague in 1887, failed to convince him that it was worth preserving, and the Quintet remained unknown until the present century, when it was published in Otakar Šourek's Complete Edition of Dvořák's works, and given its first modern performance at the Prague Conservatoire in March 1922.[10]

No doubt disappointed by his failure to achieve a worthwhile improvement of his early Quintet, Dvořák turned at once to the composition of a further work of the same type, one which would reflect his mature mastery of the chamber style. The result was his renowned Piano Quintet in A major, Op. 81, which was completed in 1887 and published in the following year, and which has since gained recognition as one of the cornerstones of the genre. Though outwardly simple in expression, with a wealth of charming themes, vivid rhythms, and colourful scoring, the work reveals much originality in its formal construction and in the wider technical resource which it embraces. Its opening cello theme, preceded somewhat 'unclassically' by two bars of piano introduction, provides a significant arch shape which is traceable as a linking factor in nearly all the first movement's subsequent ideas, despite their apparent variety of expression (see Ex. 20a–c). Very striking is the constant emphasis on the minor mode, both for incidental colouring in the first subject group, and for the principal tonality (C sharp minor) of the entire, marvellously repetitive, second subject group. Indeed, when the five successive statements of the second theme return in F sharp minor in the recapitulation, after a truncated first group, it takes a massive recall of the opening idea during the last twenty-five bars, for-

---

[10] O. Šourek (ed.), Antonín Dvořák, *Piano Quintet, Op. 5*, in *The Complete Edition of Dvořák's Works*, ser. iv, vol. 11 (Prague, 1959).

Ex. 20. Dvořák, Piano Quintet in A, Op. 81
(a), (b), and (c) 1st movement
(d) 3rd movement

tissimo, with the full ensemble, to restore the centrality of the basic A major tonic.

After the intense lyricism of the exposition, the problem of providing a cogent development section is strikingly surmounted. Following the repeat sign at the end of the exposition, the 'second-time' continuation carries forward the dramatic energy of the previous fortissimo climax for a further four bars, before starting to sink, both in tonality and dynamics, towards D major for a return of the original arch phrase. And this, directed increasingly flatwise by successive overlapping entries on the piano, viola, cello, and, eventually, violin, marks the beginning of a series of imaginative reworkings of each of the movement's principal ideas in turn. Very powerful are the results achieved by antiphonal treatment, for example at 13 bars after $\boxed{F}$ where a two-bar section of the second subject, on the strings, is pitted against an equivalent fragment of the main subsidiary theme of the first group, on the piano; and by the exciting method of approaching the recapitulation. In a manner which parallels the equivalent, though distinctly more sombre, passage in the first movement of his D minor Symphony, Op. 70, an extended crescendo leads to a vivid climax at letter ⌈I⌉, where, over 6/4 harmony in A major (approached through an augmented 6th on F), the piano provides a largamente version of the main arch theme as a grand seven-bar lead back to the long-awaited moment of recapitulation.

For the middle movements, the composer turns to two of his favourite Slavonic forms, the Dumka and the Furiant, but treats neither in an entirely usual fashion. In the slow movement, for example, the swings of mood between sadness and exultation, by which the musical form of the Dumka parallels its original Ukrainian folk-ballad models, are less pronounced than usual. Although vivid contrast is provided by the central Vivace, with its lively rhythms in 2/8 time and rapid changes of key, the second and fourth episodes are too suave to conform wholly to the accepted pattern. In fact the large number of sections the composer employs, and their distribution within the movement, suggest that he may have taken as his model the second movement, 'In modo d'un marcia', of the Schumann Piano Quintet.[11] The following comparison of the outline shapes of the two movements shows the extent of their structural similarity:

Schumann	Dvořák
Introduction: 2 bars	Introduction: 4 bars
A Marcia (i): C minor	A Dumka (i): F sharp minor
B Episode I: C major	B Episode I: D major
A Marcia (ii): C minor	A Dumka (ii), with Intro.:
C Agitato: F minor (derived	F sharp minor
from Marcia)	C Vivace: F sharp major
A Marcia (iii): C minor	(derived from Intro.)
B Episode I: F major	A Dumka (iii): F sharp minor
A Marcia (iv): F/C minor	B Episode I: F sharp major
Coda: 8 bars	A Dumka (iv), with Intro.:
	F sharp minor
	Coda: 13 bars

The paired themes in Dvořák's first main section, initially shared between viola and piano, provide opportunities for a variety of

---

[11] D. Beveridge, 'Dvořák's Piano Quintet, Op. 81: The Schumann Connection', in *Chamber Music Quarterly* (Spring, 1984), 2.

scoring in the subsequent reprises which is hardly possible with Schumann's simpler thematic material. But it is interesting to notice how, in each movement, the second repeat of the A section includes a countersubject drawn from its preceding fast section. In Schumann's case this involves the vivid opening pattern of the Agitato section, set for violin and cello in octaves against the march theme on the viola; and in Dvořák's, a series of descending triplets in the piano accompaniment taken from the falling triad at the start of his Vivace. Furthermore the melodic patterns of the two fast sections, the source of the 'borrowings', are themselves both derived from earlier material, Schumann's from his march theme and Dvořák's from his introduction.

The third movement is described as a 'Scherzo', with the term 'Furiant' included only in parentheses, as if to acknowledge that it lacks some typical features of the folk-dance. Particularly absent is the characteristic alternation of 2/4 and 3/4 metres, an effect usually achieved by accenting the last beat of fast triple-time bars, with a tie over the bar-line. The movement is, nevertheless, one of great brilliance, which conceals beneath its exciting melodic exterior many subtle details of construction. These include the arched countermelody on the viola from bar 9 which recalls the curved shape of the first movement's opening theme (see Ex. 20d); the overlapping entries at bars 74 and 94 which contract the normal four-bar phrasing; and at bar 141, the ingenious augmentation of the first violin's four-note figure in bars 2 and 3 of the main theme to form the principal subject of the 'trio'. Notable examples of scoring include echoing violin notes at the first and last appearances of the 'trio' theme; the same theme's setting in cross-rhythms, with 'Puccinian' sonority, from bar 192;[12] and the sparkling passage at bars 50–7, where the string countertheme is gradually displaced from the top of the texture by the piano as it stretches the main theme up to a′′′′, the highest available note on the seven-octave keyboard of the time.

With its vigorous upbeat start, the principal idea of the rondo finale is of a type which seems positively to demand some brief

[12] The low-pitched viola theme, doubled by repeated notes in the piano left hand, and at the octave above by triplets in the right hand, the second violin pizzicato, and the continuously repetitive patterns, provide a texture which curiously anticipates Puccini's 'oriental' style, as found for example at Sharpless's first entry, with 'Quanto alla discendenza', in Act 1 of *Madama Butterfly*.

introductory material. Other examples abound in 19th-century music, from the opening of the last movement of Beethoven's 'Eroica' Symphony onwards. Dvořák, the cunning tactician, draws his preface from the last four notes of the theme itself, and with it creates what sounds like, and later actually proves to be, a typical approach passage heralding the return of the rondo theme. Also, he arranges for his apparently insignificant introductory fragments to feature prominently later in the movement, both as a means of building transitions and, after the first rondo reprise, as important contributors to the development section. At letter $\boxed{F}$, the movement is reinvigorated by a fugato, with successive entries by the three upper strings followed by the cello and piano in octaves. Based on a minor version of the opening theme, it tends—and may well be intended—to sound mock-serious in its exuberant context, but builds strongly to the final, climactic rondo return. During the coda, following his frequent practice, Dvořák withdraws briefly, in tempo, pitch, and dynamics, in order to enhance the brilliance of the movement's final bars, much as Beethoven does at the end of his first 'Rasumovsky' Quartet and his last Violin Sonata, Op. 96 in G major. In the resulting stillness, fragments of the main theme, marked '*pp* tranquillo', are preceded by two eight-bar chordal passages in which 'echoing' notes on the half-bar are provided by the first violin and subsequently by the piano. These, in a curious, but unmistakably intentional, way, recall the treatment accorded to the 'trio' theme in the preceding movement, and in the process achieve the effect of a cyclic return, not of a melody, but simply of an unusually distinctive piece of scoring.

Like Schumann before him, though less impetuously, Dvořák followed his highly successful Piano Quintet with a Piano Quartet, his Op. 87 in E flat, completed two years later in 1889. Although equally grand in structure and refined in technique, this later work lacks some of the obvious melodic charm of its predecessor and, at the inevitable expense of its popularity, replaces immediate surface attractiveness with greater subtlety of design. A degree of complexity is evident from the opening bars of the first movement, where the main theme, on the strings in octaves, contains an intrusive C♭ (the flat submediant, notated as B♮) which creates an immediate sense of ambiguity between major and minor modes, an ambiguity compounded by the piano's lively answering phrase

Ex. 21. Dvořák, Piano Quartet in E flat, Op. 87, first movement

with its emphasis on the flat mediant, G flat major, and the minor dominant, B flat minor (see Ex. 21). Not until bar 26 is the mode settled, at least temporarily, by a fortissimo restatement of the principal idea, in the tonic major and shorn of its equivocal Cb. Subsequently, to counterbalance this bias towards flat keys, the song-like second theme is set in G major (the major mediant), on the bright, sharp side of the home tonic; and in an inspired move, it returns in the recapitulation (preceding the first subject) in a clear B major—cunningly modified by further leanings on the flat submediant (G♮), high on the cello—before moving in the most graceful of modulations back to E flat major for its restatement. In a delayed reprise, the first theme returns on the piano at letter N, in its plain diatonic form, with pounding figuration on the upper strings and an elaborate new countertheme, with trills, on the cello in its deepest register. The ambiguous C♭/B♮, however, after lurking in the background, reappears most tellingly during the coda in an expressive passage, marked 'Poco sostenuto e tranquillo' (yet another 'reculer pour mieux sauter' move to enhance the vigour of the final bars), where the first four notes of the opening theme are shared between violin and viola, playing tremolando, over chromatically related chords on the piano with pizzicato support from the cello.

The two middle movements are each notable for their wide range of expression. The opening cello theme of the slow movement, in G flat major, is set out in three short paragraphs, separated by overlapping echoes on the piano which, with a second, peaceful idea on the violin, provide an air of breadth and relaxation. At letter C, however, vivid contrast results from a tempestuous passage in C sharp minor, with upper and lower figuration on the violin (in double stopped octaves) and cello against fortissimo arpeggios on the piano. The dramatic intention is well conveyed, but in practice the richness of the overall texture tends to obliterate almost entirely the deep answering phrase on the cello. In the recapitulation the balance problem is solved by allotting both the upper and lower phrases, in octaves, to the piano, but at some inevitable expense of variety in the scoring. In the third movement, a graceful Bohemian dance in waltz tempo, contrast is provided by a lively middle section in which persistent dotted rhythms build repeatedly to powerful climaxes. 'Zigeuner' features are apparent at bar 21, where the piano's theme contains a descending augmented second over an open-fifth drone bass (recalling the third, sotto voce, section in Chopin's B flat Mazurka, Op. 7 No. 1), and in the final reprise of the principal theme, where high-pitched, tremolando decoration on the piano against pizzicato strings provides an effective imitation of a cimbalom.

The contest between major and minor modes is given a new slant in the finale, where E flat minor is chosen as the principal key, with G flat major (or its enharmonic equivalent) for the second subject group. In fact it is not until very late in the movement (at letter N, during the recapitulation) that the major tonic (with its appropriate key signature) is eventually restored. The general character of the movement is well established by its vigorous opening theme, set in bare octaves, and by the 'peasant' scoring of its immediate repeat, where, in anticipation of some of

Bartók's simpler effects of colour, the melody on the viola is supported by pizzicati on the other strings (including drone fifths from the cello) and delicate repeated chords on the piano. The second subject group, surprisingly, has no less than six distinct sections, the first, third and sixth of which explore a single, vigorous, melodic pattern, while the remaining three provide smoothly lyrical counterparts to the opening theme of the movement. Thus, despite the closed nature of the individual passages, each of which is approached through a perfect cadence, and the contrasts they display between robustness and gentleness of expression, the composer's control over the organic growth of his material is never in jeopardy. At the end, during a richly-scored coda, the sudden intervention of a chord of C flat major (11 bars from the end) provides not only a splash of colour but also a clear reminder of the intrusive B♮/C♭ which contributed so tellingly to the ambiguity of mode at the start of the whole work.

Amongst Dvořák's immediate successors, the three who added most significantly to the keyboard chamber repertoire, each with a piano quartet and quintet, were Josef Suk, Vítežslav Novák, and Zdeněk Fibich. The two works by Suk—his A minor Piano Quartet of 1891, the year in which he completed his basic studies at the Prague Conservatory, before proceeding to specialize in chamber music, and his G minor Piano Quintet, Op. 8 of 1893— were written before his twentieth birthday, and reveal an understandable immaturity of style. Dedicated to Brahms, the Quintet is basically Germanic in conception, but with melodic and harmonic features, together with an opulence of scoring, which betray unmistakably its Czech roots. Novák's A minor Piano Quintet appeared in 1896, the year in which he first visited Moravia and began the special study of Moravian and Slovakian folk-music which influenced much of his later work.[13] Folk elements are apparent in the narrow range and repetitive style of many of the

---

[13] A strange feature of the work is an alteration to the last seven bars of the first movement, made by the composer for a new edition in 1944, 48 years after its initial publication. In the original, very striking, version the final cadence was approached through chords of F minor (= E sharp minor) and C sharp major and minor. The alteration involved the placing of a bass D♮ below the F minor chord (to create a secondary seventh), the insertion of a new, rising bass line (G♯,A♯,B, B♭,A) in the antepenultimate bar, and the replacement of the tonic major chords in the final bars by minor ones. As a result the overall harmonic effect is greatly strengthened without in any way damaging its basic originality.

Quintet's principal ideas, and in the four-square rhythm of the 'motto' theme, marked 'Slovácky', at the start of the finale. A further ethnic element is his use of 'an old Bohemian Minnelied from the 15th century', entitled 'Eliško, milá, srdečná' ('Eliska, dear, affectionate'), as a basis for the set of seven variations which forms the central movement. In the finale a recall, shortly after the start, of the Andante theme from the first movement reveals the composer's interest in cyclic organization, later to be explored more extensively in his symphonic poems. The third Czech composer, Fibich, was trained principally at the Leipzig Conservatoire, for some three years from 1865, and, possibly for this reason, reveals less independently nationalist traits. His relatively small amount of chamber music, dating mainly from early in his career, includes a Piano Quartet in E minor, and a delightful Quintet in D major, of 1893, for the unusual combination of piano, violin, cello, clarinet, and horn. Inspired by the special nature of this ensemble, the composer provides a light, open texture, containing much solo and dialogue writing for the individual instruments, backed by delicate chromatic harmony. Although the influence of Schumann is constantly apparent, the two inner movements, a Largo of unusual construction, part rondo and part variations, and a Scherzo, of vigorous, peasant-dance character, marked 's divokým humorem' ('with wild humour') both show distinctively Czech characteristics. Most clearly 'nationalistic' in manner, however, is the final section of the slow movement, a hymnic melody in B flat, which returns *grandioso* in the finale to provide an impressive climax.

A further Slavonic work of unusual interest is the Piano Quintet in G minor, Op. 34 by Juliusz Zarębski, the most enterprising Polish composer of the second half of the century. After studies in Vienna and St Petersburg he came, in 1874, at Rome and Weimar, under the tutelage of Liszt, who is reputed to have regarded him as his 'favourite pupil'. During 1885, the year of his untimely death, Zarębski and some string players amongst his colleagues at the Brussels Conservatoire played through the Quintet to Liszt (the trusted arbiter in his time of so many piano quintets!) who is said to have remarked upon it in a particularly complimentary way. A substantial composition, in four movements, the work has a rich, but not over-indulgent, piano part, with intricately woven string contributions in which a balance between chordal and

imitative writing is carefully preserved. Folk elements are particularly evident in the Scherzo, not only in the drumming chords at
the start (comprising superimposed fifths, C–G and G–D, on the
strings) but also in the charmingly four-square string theme over
continuous G flat arpeggios on the piano, in the first episode. An
unusual feature is provided at the start of the Presto finale, where
the Scherzo theme returns in a brief introduction, as the first of a
number of such recalls which feature later in the movement.

The cyclic transfer of themes evident in the works by Fibich,
Novák, and Zarębski, is a technique which was increasingly
employed by composers of all European nationalities during the
second half of the nineteenth century. Although undoubtedly
effective, not simply as a display of ingenuity, but also as a means
of achieving unity in multi-movement works, it too easily degen-
erated at the hands of some second-rank composers into a largely
mechanical device, with thematic cross-references turning up rou-
tinely in the texture like clues in a detective story. It is noticeable
that, apart from César Franck whose musical language is steeped
in the technique, the leading chamber composers of the period are
sparing in their use of the practice. Brahms and Dvořák occa-
sionally bring back the principal theme from the first movement in
the finale, the former in his B flat String Quartet, Op. 67 and
Clarinet Quintet, Op. 115, for example, and the latter in his Piano
Trio in F minor, Op. 65; while Fauré (unlike many of his contemporaries in France for whom the system became almost an obses-
sion) provides only two very limited examples, in the Scherzo of
his second Piano Quartet and the finale of his second Violin
Sonata, both intricately devised for special purposes.

Some strikingly effective instances of the transfer of themes
occur in Saint-Saëns's first major chamber composition, his four-
movement Piano Quintet in A minor, Op. 14, of 1855, composed
when he was twenty. The work opens with portentous chordal
phrases in minims on the piano, which form an obvious type of
motto theme to precede the entry of the first subject at bar 15; and
this impressive pattern returns, subsequently, at the end of the
third (Presto) movement, set against that movement's principal
theme, deep in the bass, and again, in a version in C sharp major,
towards the end of the finale, in combination with part of the
second subject from the first movement. At the same time, in
the slow movement, an accompanimental pattern (already fore-

shadowed in chromatic string phrases during the first movement's development section) is established—*pp*, leggierissimo, on the viola—which, in the minor, becomes the principal theme of the ensuing Presto. The composer's skill in handling his material is remarkable, and the work as a whole shows brilliant technical control. But, as is not infrequently the case with Saint-Saëns, it lacks truly memorable thematic ideas. Most characteristic is the Presto third movement, a Scherzo (though not so called) somewhat in Mendelssohn's 'fairy' manner, but more heavyweight and more macabre. A curious feature is the inclusion, in this movement only, of an additional part for double bass, fortunately marked 'ad lib', since its compulsory presence would make the work difficult to programme, except in conjunction with Schubert's 'Trout' Quintet or some similarly scored work. The instrument's function, which it fulfils admirably, is to give extra spring to what is already a very lively movement, either by supporting the cello line or, when it is the only stringed instrument playing, giving added weight to the piano bass.

During the 1850s and 1860s, French chamber music was fostered largely by the many music societies which were active in Paris at the time. In general their programmes were devoted more to works of German origin (which in any case enjoyed greater approbation) than to the relatively few home-grown compositions of the period. But it is likely that chamber works by such rising composers as Lalo and Saint-Saëns—particularly the latter's unpublished Piano Quartet in E flat (1853), A minor Piano Quintet (1855), and F major Piano Trio (1863)—were first performed under their auspices. It was not, however, until 1871 that a major resurgence in French instrumental music began, with the foundation by Saint-Saëns and Romain Bussine, with the active support of Massenet and Fauré, of the Société Nationale de Musique. Created under the shadow of the disastrous Franco–Prussian War, the society aimed to salve national pride by encouraging a new phase of creativity by French composers. And in the outcome the enterprise proved highly successful, providing during the next forty years or so an impetus behind the composition of numerous new works of high quality, not least in the realm of chamber music. Important additions to the particularly favoured strings and piano genres were made not only by Lalo and Saint-Saëns, but also by Castillon, Chausson, D'Indy, and most notably, César Franck and Fauré.

In 1875, in a further fine contribution to the repertoire, Saint-Saëns produced his Piano Quartet in B flat, Op. 41, one of the most successful of his chamber works. Typically restrained is the opening movement, where lyrical string melodies are presented against prevalent arpeggio figuration on the piano, and dramatic sonata conflict in the German manner is almost totally excluded. In the slow movement the strings, three octaves apart, provide a pair of five-bar melodic 'limbs' against a rhythmic ostinato on the piano and, with the scoring pattern subsequently reversed, create a type of 'organ' chorale prelude, using a neo-baroque style similar to that cultivated in the first movement of the composer's Second Piano Concerto, of 1868. Vivid contrast is presented by the ensuing movement, a feather-light scherzo in D minor, characterized once again by repeated rhythmic patterns. Two episodes separate recurrences of the scherzo, the first in B flat, during which a new fanfare-style theme adds extra rhythmic twists to the original pattern, and the second, in E flat and 2/4 time, more suave and gently humorous in expression. After each episode there are short cadenzas, one for violin marked 'ad lib' (meaning 'freely', not 'optional') and a second for the piano, both of which terminate in explosive dominant chords to herald the return of the scherzo. Thematic transfer is confined to the last movement. After a second return of the main theme, in a rondo-like structure, the composer recalls, successively, the first and second themes of the first movement, and immediately, in a new section, the 'chorale' theme from the slow movement (marked ⓐ in Ex. 22), set against the second theme from the first movement (marked ⓑ) in an ingenious, if short-lived, type of double fugue—a brief moment of testimony to the composer's remarkable skill as a contrapuntist (see Ex. 22 for an outline of the passage).

The career of Marie-Alexis, Vicomte de Castillon de Saint-Victor is curiously similar to that of Prince Louis Ferdinand, the nephew of Frederick the Great, whose compositions were surveyed in Chapter 2. Both men were of exalted lineage, both were at one time professional soldiers, both died young, the German in battle and the Frenchman of ill health resulting from wartime privations, and both were dedicated musicians with a particular love of

Ex. 22. Saint-Saëns, Piano Quartet in B flat, Op. 41, finale

chamber music. In 1870, after some unsatisfactory early studies with the composer Victor Massé, Castillon came to the attention of César Franck, and under his guidance produced, before his untimely death in March 1873, a series of effective chamber works, including a Piano Quintet in E flat, in 1870, and a Piano Quartet in G minor, in 1872. Indebted in style to Mendelssohn and Schumann, his works are notable for the quality of their thematic invention, but betray some of the structural weaknesses of their models, notably in a reluctance to develop their material without excessive repetition at different pitch levels. As one of the founders, in 1871, of the newly-established Société Nationale, Castillon came to the attention of Vincent D'Indy, who generously, though not perhaps entirely without exaggeration, declared him to be 'one of the most interesting figures among the originators of the movement which revived the cult of chamber music in France'.[14]

In 1878 D'Indy, himself, began the composition of a Piano Quartet in A minor, but the work appears to have caused him much difficulty, since it was not completed until ten years later. More characteristic is his Piano Quintet in G minor, Op. 81, of

---

[14] In the article, 'Castillon', in W. W. Cobbett, *Cyclopedic Survey of Chamber Music*, 2nd edn., 1963, vol. 1, p. 232.

1924, to which we shall turn in a later chapter. Also postponed, to enable a direct comparison to be made with Brahms's great Piano Quintet in F minor, is the most renowned Parisian chamber work of the time, the massive F minor Piano Quintet by César Franck, of 1879.

During the period from the 1870s onwards into the following century, the largest contribution to French chamber music in general, and to the genres with which this book is concerned in particular, was that of Gabriel Fauré. Concentrating almost exclusively on works for piano and strings, he provided between 1876 and 1921 two examples each of the violin sonata, the cello sonata, the piano quartet, and the piano quintet; and during the remaining years to his death in 1924, a single piano trio and a single string quartet, this last being his only work for strings alone.[15]

The Piano Quartet in C minor, Op. 15, was composed between 1876 and 1879, and first performed at a Société Nationale concert in Paris on 14th February 1880, with Ovide Mussin (violin), Louis van Waefelghem (viola), M. Mariotti (cello), and the composer as pianist. Remarkable equally for its dramatic vitality and lyrical charm, the work reveals the composer, early in his career, apparently revelling in the processes of creation—however prolonged and arduous they may actually have been. The vigorous opening string phrase, punctuated by 'Elgarian' off-beat chords on the piano, provides rhythmic cells which dominate much of the first movement; and at the same time, it implants a modally inflected step to the flat leading-note (prefiguring the opening of Debussy's G minor String Quartet), which, if only as a gesture, loosens at once the grip of pure 'Austro–German' diatonicism. Contrast with the agile opening idea is provided by a smoothly linear second subject, introduced at bar 38 by the viola and echoed in imitative sequences by the violin and cello, at one-bar intervals, and by the piano, dolce, in its higher register. Wholly characteristic of the composer's naturally contrapuntal mode of thought is the linking (from bar 116, during the wide-ranging development) of this second subject with the opening theme in one of its many lyrical transformations. Unceasingly active, the piano combines pliant background figuration with melodic and imitative contri-

---

[15] See J. B. Jones, 'The Piano and Chamber Works of Gabriel Fauré', Univ. of Cambridge diss. 1974.

butions, everywhere crafted with skill and imagination; while the strings, which rarely provide simple accompaniment patterns, are treated as an integrated three-part ensemble with their individual lines linked contrapuntally. And as a result the delicate motivic threads stand out with perfect clarity, despite the overall fullness of sonority achieved.

The opening pizzicato chords of the Scherzo establish an ostinato pattern against which the piano delivers its glittering six-bar theme, charmingly distributed, on its restatement, between the left and right hands, an octave apart. At bar 19, the strings introduce a new, duple-time arrangement of the theme, and after an argument with the piano about which is the 'correct' version, agree to a compromise at bar 52, where the violin and piano adopt 6/8 time and the lower strings 2/4. Not to be outdone, however, the piano provides a further, even more rudimentary, version at bar 106, to which the strings only grudgingly accede. Typical of the composer's rich harmonic palette is the repeated, very Debussyan, alternation, during the last paragraph of the Scherzo, of the tonic, E flat major, with an augmented sixth chord on its flat submediant, to provide a recurrent tint of a darker shade. In the middle section the piano, after two exploratory phrases, settles to repeated two-bar patterns, containing triplet figuration which recalls the essence of the original scherzo idea; and against this the muted strings provide a hymnic theme, in B flat but strongly modal in flavour, with a continual bias towards the flat leading-note and flat mediant. The concept is simple but strikingly original, and may well have provided a model for the equivalent section in the 'Pantoum' (scherzo) movement of the Piano Trio by Ravel, Fauré's most famous pupil.

The Adagio, again set, rather surprisingly, in the basic tonic key, provides a mood of rapt serenity. Following a preludial opening, with ascending scalic motifs over the basic interval of a fifth, a central melody in A flat is presented from bar 27 by the violin, and achieves breadth and intensity through the interlinking, over a colourful harmonic background, of many short two- and four-bar phrases, ascending and descending. Strangely persistent is the piano's rocking chordal accompaniment during which, for no less than twenty-eight bars, alternating triplet and duplet semi-quaver patterns continue unchanged, even when the right hand provides an occasional melodic surface. Eventually both earlier

[handwritten marginal note: constant melodic elements reconfigured in various metres]

sections return, the original 'preludial' idea, discreetly, through a secondary seventh on D against fleeting demi-semiquavers on the piano, and the exalted central theme, now in C minor, in a most beautiful shortened version for the piano, with a sustained chordal accompaniment on the strings, as a peaceful, finely focused, coda.

The movement which now stands at the end of the work is not the finale heard at the first performance in Paris in 1880, but one substituted by the composer in 1883, before the work's eventual publication a year later.[16] Whether it is a revised version of the original piece or a new composition is unknown, since no copy of the earlier finale has survived. Growing unobtrusively from the quiet ending to the Adagio, the movement opens pianissimo, with triplet-quaver arpeggios on the piano in 9/8 time, against which the viola takes the opening scalic idea of the previous movement and extends it upwards, in trochaic dotted rhythms, to a full octave. At bar 95, following a powerful climax with the strings in octaves against richly scored piano writing, a song-like second subject in E flat, on the viola, emerges from its surroundings, the Schubertian elegance of which is underlined by the colourful passing modulations it encompasses—through D flat major, E (= F flat) major and its dominant, C major and minor, to a dominant seventh in B flat preceding its return at bar 116 (see Ex. 23). In a surprising move at the start of the development (bar 158), the composer eliminates his dancing quaver patterns and substitutes a limping theme on the piano, against which the strings at low pitch provide growling dotted rhythms, derived from an earlier climactic point at bar 39. The intention is clearly to provide contrast, but in the absence of the preceding rhythmic drive, the result is too static to be fully convincing. Fifty bars later, however, a return of the second subject in an expanded form on the cello, and two bars later, of the continuous triplet patterns on the piano, renew the original onrush nearly to the end. 'Nearly', because Fauré, unusually for him, brings everything to a halt at bar 342 and, over a last inversion dominant seventh in D flat, provides a tiny arpeggio cadenza, marked 'a piacere', for the piano. This somewhat Lisztian device is perhaps unduly conventional, but none the less charming in its context; and by providing a temporary moment of repose, it

---

[16] See R. Orledge (ed.), preface to Gabriel Fauré, First Piano Quartet, Op. 15 (Eulenburg minature score No. 1403, 1979).

Ex. 23. Fauré, Piano Quartet in C minor, Op. 15, finale

marvellously enhances the brilliance of the ensuing coda, with its final bars, set in the major over an extended tonic pedal.

The second Piano Quartet, Op. 45 in G minor, was first performed in Paris, at a Société Nationale concert, on 22 January 1887, and published later in the same year, with a dedication 'À Hans de Bülow'. Little is known about the circumstances surrounding its composition, but it is likely to have been completed in 1886, the same year as César Franck's Violin Sonata. In terms of technique and maturity of style it represents a considerable advance on its predecessor; but with its greater depth of expression and more intense rhythmic energy, it has less obvious appeal than the earlier work, and is generally less 'comfortable' in the thoughts and feelings it conveys. The first movement is launched, typically enough, with rustling arpeggio patterns on the piano, against which the principal subject, a fine, arching theme in a bold declamatory style, but with latent contrapuntal possibilities, is presented by the whole string ensemble, with the viola and cello, in unison, an octave below the violin. As in the earlier work, modality is again immediately in evidence, not only in the flat leading-note at the start of the theme, but also in the Phrygian A flats which colour its progress. The second subject appears already in bar 20, a calm transformation of the opening theme of the movement, set for solo viola in two matching phrases, with chordal piano accompaniment; and between these phrases, as if to make the thematic relationship even more plain, the piano interjects with grand effect the initial sweeping idea of the first subject. Immediately after, with maximum unity of conception in mind, the composer provides a diminution of the viola's theme, as a further, and eventually more enduring, contribution to the second subject group. To end the exposition, a further reference, in E flat, to the opening limb of the first subject leads to a solemn, and seemingly irrelevant, new idea on the two lower strings, marked '*pp* molto tranquillamente', which ushers in the development. At bar 109, however, this linking passage returns on the piano in A major, and from bar 118 becomes, in diminution and with overlapping imitations between the strings, an important element in the gradual build-up (a restoring of energy) to the point of recapitulation. After a regular reprise of the opening section, an unobtrusive change at bar 146 shifts the tonality a semitone lower, so that a return of the first version of the second subject, in the tonic major, is approached, in purely classical style, from its dominant.

The second movement, a scherzo in all but name, compares interestingly with the equivalent section in the earlier quartet. Although set in the same style and tempo, with the same time signature, and a very similar pizzicato accompaniment for its main theme on the piano, it is nevertheless very different in expression. Where the earlier scherzo was quiet, playful, and ingratiating, the one in the second quartet is loud, brittle, and violent, with a principal subject made continuously 'ungainly' by its off-beat accents and relentless left-hand arpeggio patterns. There is no central trio section; instead two returns of the scherzo theme are separated by episodes to give an overall rondo design. The two episodes are of unusual interest since they provide the first indication (continued more tenuously in the finale) that the work involves one of Fauré's rare uses of cyclic construction. His aim was clearly to continue the distinctive lines of thought engendered in the expansive opening movement into the very different context of the fierce, rebellious scherzo, and thus signal a hidden, enigmatic, relationship between the two movements. In the first episode, the strings, in octaves, introduce (from bar 51) a new, forte, version of the second subject from the first movement, set in triple-time crotchets to form strong cross-rhythms against the accented 6/8 patterns in the piano accompaniment; and in the second episode (from bar 134), a gentle metamorphosis of the first movement's powerful opening subject is set, in 2/4 time, in the strings, against the principal 'scherzo' theme on the piano, both 'sides' playing pianissimo in a sudden moment of unexpected calm. Thus, in a remarkable experiment in unification, the composer recalls his first-movement themes not only in reverse order, but also with their original dynamics and shades of expression largely exchanged. Later, at the second scherzo return, the principal theme is allotted for the first time to the strings, with canonic imitation by the viola, an octave below the violin and at the distance of a whole bar. Calm after the storm reigns eventually in a final skeletal texture, where pianissimo scales and arpeggios against a C minor chord on the strings, held for eighteen bars, bring the movement to the gentlest of endings—apart, that is, from a final, perhaps sardonic, forte chord, with all three strings using triple or quadruple stoppings to enhance the sonority.

In a letter to his wife Marie, Fauré declared that the opening of the Adagio non troppo was inspired by his recollection of the sound of bells in the evening, which, as a child, he had heard coming from the nearby village of Cadirac.[17] If so, they must have been deep and sonorous bells to judge from the low-pitched opening sections on the piano, where divided octaves, E♭ to G, tolling in the bass, form cross-rhythms against an interior quaver figure in 9/8 time. Between these sombre passages, a viola, entirely solo, meditates most tenderly with a tiny wisp of a phrase in a Dorian G minor (anticipating Vaughan Williams of the *Tallis Fantasia*); and from these slender fragments, Fauré constructs one of his most beautiful slow movements. In an overall sonata-rondo structure the opening section returns twice, each time with the 'bells' passage remodelled and rescored; and at the same time the solo viola theme from the opening is expanded, in a variety of scorings, with the utmost lyrical freedom, often in partnership with the second subject, a placid idea in E flat first heard at bar 26 on the piano. In Fauré's most exalted vein, and showing his remarkable ear for delicate scoring, is the lovely coda, starting at bar 95. The cello, muted, takes up the interior quaver figure from the opening 'bells' idea, inverts it and provides, in augmentation, an ostinato pattern in dotted crotchets, creating a new effect marvellously suggestive of muffled bells; and between each phrase the piano, using the original quaver values, inserts its own inverted version of the same figure. After six bars the upper strings enter, also muted, with the viola supporting the cello ostinato an octave above, while the violin provides yet another version, in E flat, of the original viola theme. In the piano's continuation, which involves *en passant* the Neapolitan E (= F flat) major, there results a passage of such intoxicating beauty that the composer is unable to resist repeating it complete, between bars 105 and 108 (see Ex. 24). Finally, five bars from the end, in stillness, the 'bells' on the cello swing gently out of phase with the rest of the ensemble, with accented syncopations which anticipate by a quaver the second and fourth beats of each bar.

The finale provides a further example of Fauré's moto perpetuo writing, with triplet quavers dominating the overall progress.

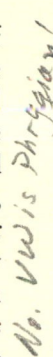

No. VIII is Phrygian!

[17] G. Fauré, *Lettres intimes* (1885–1924), ed. P. Fauré-Fremiet (Paris, 1951), 132.

Ex. 24. Fauré, Piano Quartet in G minor, Op. 45, 3rd movement

Considerably longer than the equivalent movement of the C minor Quartet, it tends to rely excessively on repetition and at times outgrows its initial impetus, for example, in bars 249–68, where the approach to the recapitulation becomes dangerously over-stretched. Two of the themes bear sufficient similarity to ones in the first movement to suggest that the composer may have in-tended, by the most indirect of means, to extend his overall cyclic plan; but the resemblance is quite slight, and may very well be coincidental. The sections in question are the Brahmsian chordal passage at bar 68, which shares its falling arpeggio shape with the 'linking' idea at the start of the development in the first movement;

and the sustained, chromatically-falling, motive on the lower strings, from bar 92, which relates loosely to some of the gentler versions of the opening theme of the whole work—for example, the one in bars 97–9 of the first movement. In practice, however, these thematic relationships, important though they may have seemed in the intensive act of composition, make little impact upon the general sense of unity in the work. It is the more customary Fauréan characteristics—the vividness of rhythm, the richness of melody and harmony, the strength of the bass lines, and the subtlety of the scoring—which prove to be, overwhelmingly, the determining factors.

One of the most independent of nationalists, Fauré stood remarkably aloof from the changing fashions of his time. During the earlier part of his career, he was influenced hardly at all by the Wagnerian rhetoric which proved so alluring to most of his contemporaries; and after the turn of the century he remained as impervious to the radical experimentation of the times as to the hypersensitive impressionism of the Debussy era. Although he had many pupils he had few successors or imitators. In its uniqueness his musical language afforded to sincere admirers little or no scope for logical extension, while to imitators it provided an avenue only to the opprobrium due to the plagiarist. Nevertheless, as one of the largest contributors of the period to the chamber repertoire, he was able to point the way towards a new refinement and technical poise in this branch of composition, which was to prove immensely influential in shaping the modernist approaches of succeeding generations of composers. After 1900, with a deepening of his style, his music turned increasingly towards a more private, inward-looking, world of thought, and this, unfortunately, has tended to limit its appeal, particularly outside his native country. However, the qualities of purity of texture, clarity of expression, and finely-controlled technique which characterize much of his later work— not least the two piano quintets, to be considered later—are, to the sympathetic listener, precisely the ones through which the essential nature of chamber composition is most fully realized.

4
The Ascendancy of Brahms

A N intense capacity for self-criticism, and what Schumann called 'another genius—that of modesty',[1] were typical of Brahms from the start of his career. His modesty, though often well concealed from the outside world, is evidenced by the letters he wrote to his closest and most knowledgeable friends—Joachim, Clara Schumann, Elisabeth von Herzogenberg, and Theodor Billroth—repeatedly seeking advice and assurance about his latest compositions as they progressed;[2] and his self-criticism, by his destruction of numerous early works which failed to satisfy him, among them a Phantasie Piano Trio in D minor, a String Quartet in B flat, and a Violin Sonata in A minor, all written before 1853. It was not, therefore, ease of creation, but a hard-won maturity that provided him with the sovereign technical command, apparent eventually over the whole range of his published chamber music. With the loss of his apprentice works there now remain few clues to the nature of his early difficulties—none, certainly, comparable to those afforded by the sketch-books of Beethoven, or the uncompleted manuscripts of Schubert. But there are two works, from a later period, which provide valuable insights. One is the Piano Trio in B major, Op. 8, which, after initial publication in 1854, was substantially recomposed thirty-five years later, as a dedicated act of rescue for a much-loved, but flawed, early work; and the other the third of his piano quartets, Op. 60 in C minor, of 1875, which was based in part on a version (possibly incomplete) in C sharp minor, written some twenty years earlier and discarded at

---

[1] From his article, 'Neue Bahnen' ('New Paths'), in the *Neue Zeitschrift für Musik* (Leipzig, 28 Oct. 1853), in which he wrote of the young Brahms, 'May the highest Genius strengthen him; this may well be expected because he is also possessed of another genius—that of modesty.'

[2] 'I beg for some really severe criticism', he wrote to Joachim in respect of the first piano concerto; and with regard to its orchestration, 'I am still very ignorant, and I don't know how to help myself.' Letter of February, 1858, quoted in Hans Gal, *Johannes Brahms: His Work and Personality*, trans. J. Stein (London, 1963), 115–16.

the time, but saved from immediate destruction because of its deep personal significance. Unfortunately, the original version of the quartet has long since disappeared, and inevitably no precise details of its reconstruction can be adduced; but documentary evidence, mainly in the form of letters, provides background information of much interest, to which we shall return later.

The earliest mature examples of the composer's keyboard chamber style are the Piano Quartets, Op. 25 in G minor and Op. 26 in A major, which date from 1861–2. As determined particularly by their opening movements, the two works show strong contrasts of expression: the first, resolute and intense, and the second, warm, lyrical, and relaxed. Working in each on a grandly 'symphonic' scale, Brahms achieves a wholly individual blend of structural logic and complex motivic development, the nature of which appears at times to have puzzled even the most enlightened of his contemporaries.[3] Joachim, in a letter of 15 October 1861, questioned the originality of the G minor Quartet's first movement and suggested that 'its various irregularities of rhythmic construction' were unsuited to their context. It is not known whether any alterations were made in response to this; but if not, it is difficult to see what could have troubled Joachim about the rhythms, which are in fact simpler in this movement than in many others by Brahms. More to the point might have been the impressive 'irregularities' in the overall key pattern, at which Clara Schumann hinted, when she declared (in a letter of 29 July 1861) that the movement was 'more D major than G minor'. Its peculiarity lies in the large amount of dominant tonality which the composer employs in the exposition, involving some two-thirds of the total number of bars, which results from an early move, at bar 50, to D minor for the start of the second subject group, and to D major, only thirty bars later, for an extended variant of the same idea. Unusual also, from a structural viewpoint, is the start of the recapitulation, where the first-group themes return in reverse order: first, a subsidiary 'limb' of the opening subject (originally at bar 11 of the piano part) in the tonic major; then a 'false' recapitulation, fortissimo, in D minor; and finally, seven bars later, the 'real', much delayed, reprise of the first subject in the tonic

[3] W. Frisch, *Brahms and the Principle of Developing Variation* (Berkeley and Los Angeles, 1984).

minor. The second theme returns in its major version only, and set with wonderful richness of effect in the submediant, E flat major, to be followed, from bar 303, by an independent tranquillo passage for the strings alone, which, with a further version incorporating the piano, strikingly enlarges the perspective of the movement as a whole.

In the first movement of the A major Quartet attention is caught at once by the Schubertian flow of its melodies, presented largely in pairs with contrasts of scoring, and by the manner in which its themes and motifs grow organically from each other.[4] Like its predecessor, the second work starts with the piano alone, presenting as its first idea an undulating triplet figure which is destined to play a major role in later developments. Then, after four bars, the cello contributes, as its 'paired' answer, a smooth melodic line, headed by a variant of the undulating pattern. Subsequently, scoring contrast is provided in an immediate repeat, during which the opening idea is entrusted to the strings alone (in rich harmony, with violin double-stoppings), and the cello's answering phrase to the piano, in octaves, a fourth higher. More striking still is the use of interconnected ideas at bar 37, where a pair of two-bar motifs, (x) and (y), presented in succession on the strings, against a descending chordal pattern on the piano, are immediately telescoped into a single two-bar pattern, with the first motif, (x), allotted to the strings and the second, (y), simultaneously, to the piano (see Ex. 25a). Thus, within his first large paragraph, Brahms provides an epitome of his mature chamber style, in which thematic interchange, variety of scoring, counterpoint, and the logical evolution of ideas all play a vital role. The manner in which themes emerge progressively from their predecessors can be seen in Example 25b, where a number of individual motifs from the second subject group are set side by side for comparison. The initial major-key phrase at bar 61 is varied at bar 65, returns in the minor at bar 77, and is inverted from bar 82, with emphasis thrown progressively on the three-note motif marked (z); this figure is then isolated, and after treatment in imitation between strings and piano, leads from bar 93 into a new theme on the strings, the

---

[4] See J. Webster, 'Schubert's Sonata Form and Brahms's First Maturity', II, *Nineteenth Century Music*, vol. 3, pt. 1 (July 1979), 52, for a discussion of Schubert's influence on Brahms.

Ex. 25. Brahms, Piano Quartet in A, Op. 26, 1st movement

fourth of the second group's principal melodic ideas. Finally the (z) pattern functions as an important element in the codetta, which, from bar 119, straddles both first and second time bars at the end of the exposition.

The second movement of the G minor Quartet was originally described as a scherzo, but the composer later substituted the term Intermezzo, with the tempo marking 'Allegro, ma non troppo'. It thus forms an early example of the relatively subdued type of scherzo-substitute which Brahms was to make particularly his own—for example, in each of his symphonies except the last. As in parallel movements in various of his other chamber works, the mood established is one of mystery and suspense, enhanced in this instance by the use of the minor mode, muted strings, and almost continuously soft dynamics. At the same time a curious ambiguity of expression is created from the start, where (with the piano temporarily silent) pulsating triplet quavers on the cello suggest agitation, while the melodic surface, with violin and viola in parallel sixths, expresses gentleness and calm.[5] The composer's constant aim of combining variety with unity is wonderfully realized in the central trio section. Set in A flat, and marked animato, it adapts many of the principal rhythms of the 'scherzo' to new melodic shapes, and substitutes for the repeated notes of the opening section a new wavering triplet-quaver line, first on the piano and later in the strings, to achieve a high degree of integration.

The equivalent movement in the second quartet, placed third, is entitled Scherzo, unequivocally, though its gait is hardly less sedate than that of its predecessor. Broad and open-hearted in manner, its structure—which Joachim rather strangely described as 'compact' (konzentriert)—comprises, together with that of its Trio, two miniature sonata movements, each with a second subject and, within the overall scale, a relatively extended development section. Once again, unifying devices are much in evidence, for example in the way in which the second subject of the Trio, from bar 233, reproduces exactly, but in new melodic terms, the rhythm of the opening theme of the Scherzo. Yet where normal thematic repeats occur, they are rarely exact, variety being achieved by fresh counterthemes and accompaniments, or by changes in scoring. The Trio, in addition to its sonata characteristics, presents a striking example of antiphony between piano and strings, with answering phrases at the distance of a whole bar which provide for the simplest 'follow-my-leader' type of canon.

The placing of the slow movements in relation to their scherzo-type fellows is not a matter of whim, but one of obvious importance to the expressive scheme of each work as a whole. In the case of the G minor Quartet the subdued character of the Intermezzo provides a perfect backcloth to the rich colouring and expansive style of the Andante which follows, while, in the second work, the meditative style of the slow movement, and particularly the dark tensions of its closing bars, find apt release in the gracious, uncomplicated manner of the ensuing Scherzo. The large-scale Andante con moto of the earlier quartet is deployed on broad ternary lines, with varied, and at times subtly disguised,

[5] The violin melody is a transposed version of the so-called 'Clara' theme—a descending curve, originally involving the notes C, B, A, G♯, and back to A—which Schumann had devised and used in many contexts, such as the openings of his A minor Piano Concerto and D minor Symphony. A further significant use of the theme is found in the opening bars of Brahms's C minor Piano Quartet (see p. 92).

Ex. 26. Brahms, Piano Quartet in G minor, Op. 25, 3rd movement

repeats of the principal themes in each of its sections. At bar 40, for example, in what appears to be a simple transition, with accompanimental arpeggios on the piano, the whole texture is underpinned by the opening phrase of the main theme in octaves in the left hand of the piano part (see Ex. 26). The middle section, a slow march in dotted rhythms on the piano, with supporting 'fanfares' in octaves on the upper strings, must surely have been one of the main features which prompted Schoenberg to make his somewhat bizarre orchestral arrangement of the work. Starting pianissimo in C major, it returns with dramatic suddenness, fortissimo, in A flat major, and after a short canonic transition, in an even more majestic manner, in C major, with the original piano and strings scoring reversed. Following a recurrence of the transitional passage, C major is retained, at bar 151, as the key for a 'false' recapitulation, before E flat is finally restored for the true reprise, at bar 168, with the main theme varied by syncopations, in a manner reminiscent of Schumann.

Similarly sectional in construction, the slow movement of the A major work is shaped as a large-scale rondo with the following pattern: A−B−A′−C(i and ii)−A′′−B′−C′(i)−A′′′−Coda, where A indicates the rondo theme and B and C its interwoven episodes. Set in E major, a key clearly associated by Brahms with lyricism and deep contemplation, the main theme is allotted initially to the piano with muted strings accompanying in pairs of slurred quavers, the second of which anticipates in each case the next melody note of the keyboard part. Both in the shape of its opening theme and the manner of its scoring, this first section points forward to 'Ihr hab nun Traurigkeit', the movement which Brahms added to his *German Requiem* in 1869, in particular the passage from bar 64 where the chorus takes up the main hymnic theme and the orchestra 'shadows' it with slurred quaver patterns. In the first episode the quavers, shaped into an undulating figure, are continued by the strings, while diminished seventh arpeggios on the piano (marked 'una corda') create an air of mystery comparable to that which Schubert achieved by similar means in his Heine setting, 'Die Stadt', of 1828. In contrast, the opening of the second episode (C′) is robust and passionate. Presented initially on the piano, in B minor, and on its return in F minor on the strings, it is continually dogged by the slurred quaver patterns which, by creating a solemn undertow, link it perpetually to the main rondo idea. Calmness, however, is restored by the subsidiary element in the second episode (Cii), a tender, deeply expressive new idea, initiated at bar 58 by the strings alone and continued in varied form by the piano, which remains untouched by any of the more sinister elements in the movement.

To some fastidious modern ears, accustomed, by more recent chamber works, to pessimistic, pianissimo endings, the barnstorming style of the G minor Quartet's rondo finale may sound over-exuberant, even crude. But, in reaching out openly to entertain his players and his audience, after the introspective manner of his earlier movements, Brahms is in fact following a perfectly respectable classical tradition, of which no more apposite example could be cited than Haydn's famous rondo 'in the Gipsies' stile' from his G major Piano Trio, Hob. XV. 25. In the Brahms movement, which is typically rich in themes, the Hungarian gypsy flavour is enhanced by the three-bar, authentically 'ethnic', phrasing common to its principal idea, and to that of its second episode at bar 155; and again by its extended, delightfully wayward, cadenza, from bar 293, initiated by the piano with a cascade of demisemiquavers over a dominant seventh, and involving sections for the string trio alone, ruminating gently, or at times more fiercely, on the various episode themes in turn.[6] Equally forthright in style, and somewhat more orthodox in structure, the equivalent movement in the A major work conceals behind its exhilarating exterior a wealth of ingenious technical detail, such as the contraction of the rhythms in bars 47–52 before the first return of the main theme, the canonic treatment between piano and violin of the second subject, at bar 106, and the use of a compressed version of the C major theme at bar 143, as a bass to the cadence theme which succeeds it, from bar 175.

The third Piano Quartet, Op. 60 in C minor, was completed, as we have seen earlier, in 1875, some thirteen or fourteen years after the two previous works and at least nineteen years later than the discarded C sharp minor sketch on which it was, in part, based. In the absence of the early draft, the manuscript of which was eventually destroyed by the composer, the extent of its relationship to Op. 60 can only be conjectured.[7] However, in this case again, documentary evidence provides some valuable clues— together, regrettably, with some conflicting evidence. In a letter to the composer, undated, but believed to be of the 24 or 25 November 1856, Joachim wrote 'I have gone through the [C sharp minor] Quartet—with its austere seriousness in the first movement, the deeply felt Andante, and the terse passion of the concise finale—*several* times, each time with *new* enjoyment', apparently indicating that, in its original form, the work had only three movements. While Clara Schumann, in her diary for 18 October of the same year, referred to the 'wonderful Adagio' in the work, suggesting perhaps that a substitute had been provided for the

[6] In Stravinsky's opinion, 'even Schoenberg stumbled in trying to transfer Brahms's piano style to the orchestra...though his realisation of the cadenza in the last movement with arpeggiated pizzicatos is a masterstroke,' *Stravinsky in Conversation with Robert Craft* (Pelican Books, 1962), 42.
[7] See J. Webster, 'The C sharp minor Version of Brahms's Op. 60', *The Musical Times* (Feb. 1980), 89.

original Andante. However, Brahms, in his own manuscript catalogue of his works, for the dates 1874/75, indicates that, while the first two movements of the final work (the Allegro and Scherzo) were taken to some extent from the early draft, the third and fourth movements (the Andante and Finale) were entirely new additions in 1875.[8] Two particular questions therefore arise. If there was no Scherzo in the original draft (as Joachim seems to suggest), what was the source for this movement in the final version? Was it a reworking of the original 'passionate' finale, or perhaps some other drafted material from the early period? And if the final version contained a newly composed Andante (as Brahms appears to indicate), what happened to Clara Schumann's 'wonderful Adagio', which has sometimes been taken, mistakenly as it appears, as the one essential feature in the final work which was retained from the basic draft?

It is unlikely now that, short of the discovery of an unknown copy of the early C sharp minor version, any simple answer to these questions can be found. Nor, indeed, is it probable that any such answer would affect the accepted view of the work, in its final published form, as a fully convincing example of mature Brahms. So thoroughly, in fact, was the composer's work of reconstruction done that, had the facts about the early draft remained entirely hidden, it is unlikely that (with the possible exception of some fleeting doubts about the Scherzo) any noteworthy discrepancies of style could have been suspected in the finished product.

Essentially tragic in manner, the work's sombre character is underlined at the start by the low-pitched phrase—another manifestation of the 'Clara' motif (see footnote 5)—with which the strings respond to the piano's opening octave C. After an even darker answering phrase, a tone lower, there emerge, from a pianissimo dominant chord, enigmatic E♮s, in pizzicato octaves from the viola and violin in turn. These, by momentarily suggesting the distant key of E minor, introduce a sense of mystery and unease, before being swept aside in a vigorous return to the original tonic. At bar 70, the second subject, in the relative major,

[8] The entry in Brahms's catalogue reads: 'Movements 1. 2 | Movements 3–4 | 1 and 2 earlier; 3, 4 Vienna, Winter [18]73–74'. Catalogue published in diplomatic transcription by A. Orel: 'Ein eigenhändiges Werkverzeichnis von Johannes Brahms', *Die Musik* xxix (1936–7), 539.

takes the unusual form of an eight-bar theme with four continuously unfolding variations in different scorings, the third of which is a minor mode version of the second. After a subdued start, the development expands the first subject stormily over a wide range of keys, before a calmer exploration of the second theme, with imitative entries, gradually builds up to a powerful return of the opening in the tonic. At bar 224, the pizzicato E♮s again emerge from the major dominant chord, but this time explain themselves by actually moving to the key of E minor, in preparation for a return of the second subject in G major. Once again, there are four variations of the second theme, the first three of which are new and the fourth a recasting of the second one from the exposition. Finally, after further brusque, almost despairing, gestures the movement ends in the atmosphere of gloom in which it started.

Little relief is afforded by the ensuing Scherzo (still in C minor), the pounding 6/8 patterns of which provide from the start a sense of urgency and disquiet. A subsidiary idea, more sedate, but marked by jagged accentuation, breaks the continuity at bar 23, after which the first theme returns with its two opening bars screwed tightly together into a single measure and leads through a long crescendo to a climax of immense power. There is no separate trio section, only a quieter central episode, a fact which has encouraged the idea that the movement may have been derived from the finale of the C sharp minor draft. Furthermore, it is in this movement alone that traces can be found of an earlier style: in its overall atmosphere of storm and stress, and its similarity to some other early scherzos, such as the one (WoO 2) in the collaborative 'Frei aber einsam' violin sonata of 1853, which was offered, together with three other movements contributed by Schumann and Albert Dietrich, in honour of Joachim.

Much interest centres on the choice of E major, the strangely distant major key on the sharpened mediant, for the slow movement. Some commentators, viewing the key as the normal mediant (or relative major) of C sharp minor, have supposed it to represent a direct survival from the original quartet draft; but this, as we have seen, flies in the face of Brahms's catalogue entry which identifies the movement as newly created in 1875. Possibly the composer intended to provide with it some link with the mysterious E♮ interventions in the first movement, but it is altogether more likely that he was simply taking as his model Beethoven's Third Piano Concerto, in which precisely the same relationship prevails between the key of the slow movement and the central tonic, and with equally impressive effect. It seems probable that the key of E major held some special significance for Brahms. Although used as a principal key in none of his major works, it is not uncommonly found in slow interior contexts where a special expression of rapt contemplation is sought—most notably in the slow movement of the First Symphony, where again it is set in relation to a basic C minor. The resultant mood, particularly in Op. 60, parallels that of the slow movement, also in E major, of Beethoven's Second Rasumovsky Quartet, which, according to Czerny's colourful account, 'occurred to him when contemplating the starry sky and thinking of the music of the spheres'.[9] 'Rapt contemplation' is certainly evident in the 16-bar cello solo, with piano accompaniment, with which the movement starts, one of Brahms's loveliest ideas, gracefully designed in two matching halves with a cadence in the dominant at the centre. Very simple in outline, but complex in detail, the movement is shaped on broad sonata lines, with a particularly rich succession of themes in its second section. Although the modulatory scheme is generally restricted, a wonderfully effective touch of colour is provided at the reprise of the opening, where, in alternating passages between piano and strings, the home tonic is approached by way of G major, C major, C minor, A flat major (notated as G sharp major), and reached finally through an interrupted (V–VI) cadence in G sharp minor (see Ex. 27).

The long opening cello solo of the slow movement is matched by an even more extensive (thirty-four-bar) violin solo at the start of the finale. With its song-like melody and continuous, thematically significant, quaver accompaniment on the piano, it points interestingly forward to the minor-key finale of the composer's G major Violin Sonata, Op. 78. Standing in close relationship to both movements, though most exactly to the sonata finale, are two of Brahms's songs, 'Regenlied' and 'Nachklang', Nos. 3 and 4 from his Op. 59 set, which act as a kind of emotional link between them. The order of composition is clear: the songs came

⁹ A. W. Thayer, *The Life of Ludwig van Beethoven*, rev. and ed. Elliott Forbes (Princeton, N.J., 1964), 408–9.

Ex. 27. Brahms, Piano Quartet in C minor, Op. 60, 3rd movement

first, in 1873, the quartet movement second, in 1874–5, and the sonata movement last, in 1878–9. It seems possible, therefore, that the apt relationship of the 'raindrops/tears' symbolism of the songs to the tragic character of the quartet may have prompted the first 'borrowing'; and that the effectiveness of its violin and piano presentation in the quartet suggested, later, a more literal appropriation of the material for the sonata. With his customary aim of achieving unity through motivic transformation, Brahms adapts the initial keyboard pattern from the start of the movement, in augmentation, for the opening of his second subject at bar 54, and follows it with a striking five-bar cadence theme, for the string trio alone, in even minims in the manner of a chorale. During a lightly scored development section a significant role is played by descending chromatic scales on the piano, an unusual feature for

Ex. 28. Brahms, Piano Quartet in C minor, Op. 60, 4th movement

Brahms, which add vividly to the air of subdued drama; and at
bar 188, in a remarkable 'false' recapitulation, the first theme
reappears, deep on the violin, in B minor—a semitone 'too low'—
while the piano provides a double diminution of it as an accompaniment (see Ex. 28). A change to the major for the second
subject group in the recapitulation offers promise of a brighter,
more hopeful, end to the work, but the original, darker mood
soon returns and a final descending chromatic scale, in octaves on
the piano, suggests nothing less than ruin and dissolution.

On Brahms's own admission, the tragic character of the quartet
is attributable to the stressful personal problems which he faced
during the 1850s, when he was working on the C sharp minor
version. In February 1854, after learning of Schumann's attempted
suicide, and subsequent confinement to an asylum, he hurried to
Düsseldorf to give comfort to his friend's grief-stricken wife; and
it is clear from surviving correspondence that, in the course of
time, he developed a powerful, but in the circumstances deeply
unhappy, romantic attraction to her, which in all likelihood was
reciprocated. In a clear reference to this—from the, presumably,
cooler perspective of 1874—he described the quartet, in a letter
to Theodor Billroth, as 'a curiosity: an illustration for the last
chapter in the life of the man in the blue jacket and yellow
waistcoat', a reference to the eponymous hero of Goethe's novel
Werther, whose agonizing love for the wife of a greatly respected
friend causes him to shoot himself. And in the following year, in a
letter to Fritz Simrock about the publication of the revised quartet,
he is even more explicit: 'On the cover', he wrote, 'you must have
a picture, namely a head with a pistol pointed at it. Now you can
form some idea of the music! I will send you my photograph for

the purpose. And since you seem to like colour printing, a blue coat, yellow breeches, and top-boots would do well.'

A curiously similar tragic theme is taken up in a chamber work by Brahms's younger contemporary, Hermann Goetz, who, after a career dogged by illness, the highpoint of which was his very successful Shakespearean opera *Der widerspenstigen Zähmung* (*The Taming of the Shrew*), died early at the age of thirty-six. The work in question is his Piano Quintet in C minor, Op. 16, which was composed in 1874, and published posthumously in 1876, almost exactly at the time that Brahms was preparing his Op. 60 Piano Quartet in its final form. Although Goetz and Brahms are known to have been on friendly terms, there is no evidence of any immediate connection between them in 1874. It is, however, strange that, in addition to writing his work in the same key as Brahms's, Goetz should have chosen also to preface it with a quotation from Goethe: 'Und wenn der Mensch in seiner Qual verstummt, | gab mir ein Gott, zu sagen, was ich leide' (And when mankind is struck dumb in its misery, a god gave me the ability to say what I suffer). The quotation, which Goetz in fact gets slightly wrong, by substituting 'was' for 'wie' in the second line, comes from Act 5, Scene 5 of Goethe's *Tasso* (1790), and relates to the play's central theme, about the way an artist, unlike humanity in general, can find solace in his special ability to give expression to his suffering—a theme as appropriate to Brahms's situation as to that of Goetz.[10] As a chamber composer, however, Goetz was no Brahms. His four-movement quintet, scored, like Schubert's 'Trout', with double bass and no second violin, follows a relatively modest classical pattern, with stylistic roots derived largely from Mendelssohn and Hummel. Suffering is expressed mainly in a sombre, low-lying, slow introduction, scored, during the first eight bars, for strings alone, which provides perhaps the nearest parallel to the mood of Brahms's Op. 60. The ensuing Allegro is charming and effective, with short, tidy sections, well-crafted scoring, and much independence between piano and strings. In conformity with its Goethe motto, progress is made from its gloomy, depressed opening to eventual challenging gestures, in-

[10] By his substitution of 'was' for 'wie' (a not uncommon error even in scholarly writings) Goetz gives a slightly false slant to the meaning. In the second line, Tasso refers not so much to his ability to describe *what* has caused his pain, as to his special, divine, gift as a poet to express *how* exquisitely he is suffering.

volving fanfare-like motifs, at the end of the last movement; but there is, finally, no major-key resolution, and hardly more sense of redemption or personal triumph over adversity than in Brahms's work.

Among the piano quartets which followed in the wake of Brahms, two attract attention because of the distinction their composers were to achieve later in other branches of composition: the Piano Quartet movement in A minor, by Mahler, and the Piano Quartet in C minor, Op. 13, by Richard Strauss. The Mahler movement is one of a number of chamber works—many of them now missing or destroyed—which the composer produced between 1876 and 1878, while studying at the Vienna Conservatoire.[11] Marked on the manuscript 'Clavierquartett—1.ten Satz', the surviving section was clearly intended as part of a full-length work. A twenty-four-bar fragment of a Scherzo in G minor, also preserved, has sometimes been regarded as a further part of the same composition, but the relationship of its key to A minor makes this improbable. Somewhat tentative both in style and structure, the surviving movement contains distinctive thematic material set in a loosely organized sonata form, notable for a curious 'intermezzo' for muted strings before the recapitulation and an eruptive solo violin cadenza before the coda. In contrast, the Strauss quartet, an opulent four-movement work, completed in 1884 when the composer was twenty, exudes the confidence of a young giant, revelling in his technical expertise and creative vigour. Brahmsian features are apparent in the recurrent passages in parallel sixths, the lilting melody at the centre of the scherzo, and more generally, in the 'cut and thrust' of the scoring. But there are also significant anticipations of Strauss's later style, in the wide melodic leaps, the range of textures employed, from the most heavily 'orchestral' to the most delicate, and the placing of powerful accents across weak parts of the bar, for example at the start of the rondo finale, where the main theme enters dramatically over a Neapolitan chord on the second quaver in 2/4 time.

Together with Dvořák's Op. 81 in A, the most renowned piano quintets of the second half of the nineteenth century are those of Brahms and César Franck, both in the key of F minor. The

[11] P. Ruzicka (ed.), G. Mahler, Piano Quartet Movement in A minor (Edition Sikorski, 800, Hamburg).

Brahms work, his Op. 34, appeared in 1864 after a protracted period of gestation, during which it underwent several transformations. Originally conceived as a string quintet with two cellos (instead of the two violas more usual at the time) it was first recast as a sonata for two pianos, on the advice of Joachim who regarded the purely string ensemble as inadequate to match the power of the music, and finally, in 1864, by a combination of elements from both previous schemes, as a piano quintet. Completed when Brahms was thirty-one, not long after his first two piano quartets, it provides a majestic example of the composer's style at its early maturity. The César Franck quintet, on the other hand, belongs to the final phase of its composer's career. Written in 1879, when Franck was fifty-seven, it was the first in the series of late orchestral and chamber works, including his *Variations Symphoniques* (1885), Violin Sonata (1886), D minor Symphony (1886–8), and String Quartet (1889), with which he may be said to have crowned his life's work.

A comparison between the two quintets reveals at once the opposing stylistic premises—of classical restraint and Romantic rhetoric—from which, by natural inclination, their composers were working.[12] Whereas Brahms accepts the traditional pattern of four contrasted movements, and bases his work on the structural and developmental procedures of Beethoven and Schubert, infused with melodic and harmonic elements of Romantic orientation, Franck, with only three movements (since there is no scherzo), adopts the freer formal procedures of Liszt, and allies them to complex phrase structures, and a harmonic palette derived largely from Wagner. These basic differences of approach are reflected also in the scoring and dynamics employed in the two works. While Brahms confines the fullness of his piano part to the style and pitch-range of the string ensemble, no doubt prompted, to some extent, by the original scoring for strings alone, Franck places little restraint on his keyboard writing, and at times sub-

---

[12] The oft-repeated anecdote that, at the first performance of the Franck Quintet, Saint-Saëns, who was acting as pianist, spurned the composer's offer of the score because of the work's 'eroticism' (perhaps suggested by Franck's alleged love for his pupil, Augusta Holmes) is hard to swallow. Any such objection would surely have surfaced long before, while Saint-Saëns was preparing his part and rehearsing with the string players—unless we are to assume that he did neither of these things.

merges his strings under powerful chordal, arpeggio, or octave passages. And similarly, while Brahms contains his dynamics within the range pianissimo to fortissimo, Franck, perhaps reflecting the tonal resources of his organ at Sainte-Clotilde, enlarges the limits at both extremes, to encompass both *ppp* and *fff*.

The openings of the two works well summarize their basic differences of style and emotional expression. Brahms begins with a double statement of his principal theme, at first in an introductory manner, with piano and strings in bare octaves and mezzoforte, and subsequently, at bar 12, after a linking passage in semiquavers based on a diminution of the original idea, with the strings, fortissimo and in octaves, supported by downwardstriding arpeggios on the piano. The effect is simple and dignified, and points forward at once towards a structure in which the individual parts are to bear a precisely planned relationship to the whole conception. Franck's opening is also introductory and well integrated, but larger and more theatrical in style. Marked 'dramatico' and fortissimo, the strings alone, in C time, launch the movement with a vigorous descending theme which leads at once into a solo piano section in 12/8 time, marked '*p* espress. poco ad lib'. The dialogue between strings and piano which ensues compares interestingly with that at the start of the composer's *Variations Symphoniques*, written some six years later, and like that later opening, recalls, as a distant model, the slow movement of Beethoven's Fourth Piano Concerto in which emphatic string phrases are set, similarly, against gentler phrases on the piano. When eventually, at bar 50, the exposition proper begins, the first section of its main theme, fortissimo, on the strings, is derived clearly from the opening bars of the introduction, while the second, in quiet dotted rhythms on the piano, is related partly to the first keyboard entry at bar 6, and partly to the shape of the approaching second subject, at bar 90.

Very different are the methods used by the two composers to attain structural unity. Although Brahms allows stylistic consistency to provide the principal unifying element, he also introduces theme transformations within movements and, more rarely, half-hidden cross-references between movements. The clearest example is provided by the second idea in the Scherzo (from bar 13) which is not only derived from a subsidiary theme at bar 23 of the first movement, but also, transformed in character, forms the

Ex. 29. Brahms, Piano Quintet in F minor, Op. 34
(a) 1st movement
(b) Scherzo
(c) Scherzo

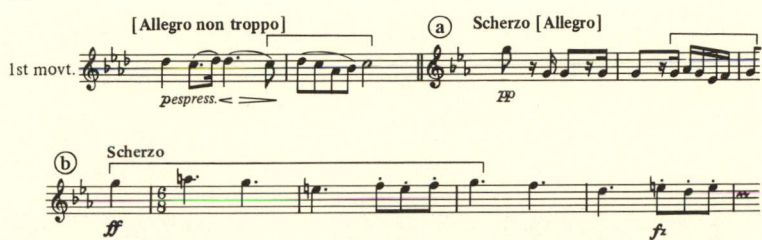

thematic material for the ensuing scherzo section (see Ex. 29). Less obvious is the role played at focal points by the interval of the minor second, ascending and descending: in the subsidiary idea at bar 57 of the first movement, for example, and as a basic constituent of the second subject of the finale from, bar 95. And equally indirect is the way in which the syncopated rhythm at the start of the scherzo, allied to an entirely new melodic surface, recurs during the final section of the last movement.

Franck, on the other hand, adopts a more transparent system of cyclic returns, one which he had established in outline as early as 1841, in the first of his Op. 1 Piano Trios. Special emphasis is placed in the quintet on the second subject of the first movement (found initially at bar 90, and given in its fullest form at bar 124), which in various guises appears as a type of 'motto' in all three movements. The theme itself consists of two four-bar phrases, the second of which is a free inversion of the first, and like others by Franck (for example, the equivalent 'motto' idea in the first movement of his Symphony, at bar 129) is restricted by its tendency to revolve around a single-note axis (see Ex. 30). Because of this, and because of its undeniably attractive melodic profile, it proves generally more amenable to repetition than to development. In the second and third movements the locations of the motto are limited and skilfully chosen. In the slow movement, for example, the piano provides two peaceful versions of the first phrase only, in D flat major, towards the end of the very beautiful middle section. While in the finale two recurrences of the complete theme—in D flat and F, respectively—occur successively in the coda, where they provide an impressive summing-up of one central emotional

Ex. 30. Franck, Piano Quintet in F minor, 1st movement

aspect of the work. In the first movement, on the other hand, an over-lavish use of the motto provides less happy results from a structural point of view. Either whole or in part, it occurs no less than eighteen times, in a wide range of keys but little modified in shape; and in the resultant patchwork structure, variety tends to be impaired by an excess of unity, and much of the natural flow of the music is lost. The other main cyclic element is a short rhythmic idea, marked '*p ma dramatico*', which first occurs in the slow movement at bar 20, on the lower strings, as a countertheme to the principal subject. Following its unobtrusive initial appearance, it returns in the finale at bar 147, as an important secondary idea and, in varying shapes and keys, features increasingly throughout the remainder of the movement. More of a motif than a theme, it lacks the appealing lyricism of the motto, and is thus able to fulfil a less conspicuous, but in many ways even more effective role in providing overall coherence to the structure.

Most nearly related in style and structure are the two slow movements, both of which are in ternary form, with deeply expressive central sections in distant keys. In Brahms's case the first section provides an extended theme in A flat, in the manner of a lullaby, which, despite being based over its 22-bar length on a single rocking pattern for the piano, contains, after its first two

bars, no exact repetitions. This leads, through a striking enharmonic modulation (at bars 31−2), to E (= F flat) major, the flat
submediant, for the richly varied middle section. In comparison,
Franck's slow movement, the most perfectly integrated of the
three, begins with a 16-bar theme in A minor for the first violin,
which is pieced together in short fragments over repeated chord
patterns in triplets on the piano. Especially noteworthy for their
precise organization are bars 5−8, the rhythmic shapes of which
mirror those of the first four bars in a free type of inversion.
Harmony of equivalent richness to that of Brahms provides an
elegant transition from A major, through F sharp major, E flat
major, via an augmented ('French') sixth, over a D♮ on the viola,
to D flat major (logically C sharp major, the major key on the
sharpened mediant) for the radiant centrepoint of the movement.

After ending his slow movement with a calculatedly tenuous
grip on A minor, Franck reasserts his hold on the key in the
remarkable opening to the finale. In a passage pointing forward
to the last movement of Ravel's String Quartet of 1902−3, the
second violin, pianissimo, provides a rapid ostinato pattern in
repeated semiquavers, centred initially around A, against which
the piano, and subsequently the other strings, moving through one
of Franck's most richly chromatic sequences, gradually re-establish
the home tonic, F major/minor, and build up the rhythmic motif
which from bar 73 is to constitute the principal subject. In the
piano accompaniment which follows, momentum is engendered
by triplet patterns which build the excitement, almost unceasingly,
to the point where the mood is at last transfigured by the final,
ppp, return of the motto theme. Altogether different is Brahms's
solution to the finale 'problem'. Following the dynamic, and at
times triumphant, manner of his scherzo, he proceeds, surprisingly,
to a mysterious slow introduction, in which 'Tristanesque' appoggiaturas, underlining the minor seconds fundamental to the work's
structure, introduce an aura of 'New German' Romanticism, which
is the nearest the composer comes to the style of Franck. The
opening ten bars, scored for strings alone, apart from an isolated
four-note contribution from the piano left hand (presumably doing
duty for a second cello entry in the original string quintet version),
lead on to a passionate descending motif, shared repeatedly between piano and strings, which recalls the 'Storm and Stress' style
of the earliest Brahms, and leads one to sense some unknown

autobiographical motivation. A further surprise is provided by the way in which the tensions built up in this introduction are frustrated by the graceful, but unusually staid, first theme of the ensuing Allegro. Not until bar 81, with an onrush of semiquavers, forte and in contrary motion, does the pent-up energy at last find release. Somewhat abnormal in structure the movement involves an exposition, containing a beautiful, rhythmically flexible, second subject, an immediate recapitulation which incorporates its own elements of development, and a long coda. This last, starting in C sharp minor, is based on a presto version of the main theme, in 6/8 time, in a manner which strikingly recalls the plan adopted by Beethoven in the last movement of his 'Archduke' Piano Trio.

Amongst those who continued over the turn of the century to explore the rich vein of 'symphonic' chamber music with piano were Reger, Dohnányi, Bartók, Webern, and Pfitzner, in closest succession to Brahms; and Chausson, Roger-Ducasse, Fauré, Florent Schmitt, and D'Indy, as the most immediate followers of César Franck. Further from the centre of Europe there were others again who adopted a broadly Brahmsian style: in England, Parry and Stanford, in Italy, Sgambati and Martucci, the major contributors to a revival of abstract instrumental composition in that country, and in Norway, Christian Sinding, whose E minor Quintet won widespread renown and prompted the young Sibelius to compose a work of a similar nature. While amongst those who took a more independent line were Arensky and Taneyev in Russia, Frank Martin in Switzerland, and Granados and Turina in Spain.[13]

The most prolific, but also, arguably, the most problematic, chamber composer at the turn of the century was Max Reger, who inherited from Brahms a deep reverence for the German classical tradition, the forms and techniques of which he sought to reinvigorate in modern terms. In addition to a clarinet quintet, a string quintet, violin and cello sonatas, and six string quartets, his output includes a piano trio, two piano quartets, in D minor and A

---

[13] Amongst works not discussed elsewhere in this survey are: G. Sgambati (Piano Quintet in F minor, Op. 4, 1866; Piano Quintet in B flat, Op. 5, 1876): G. Martucci (Piano Quintet, Op. 45, 1878): C. H. H. Parry (Piano Quartet in A, Op. 77, 1879): E. Granados (Piano Quintet in G minor, 1898): J. Roger-Ducasse (Piano Quartet in G minor, 1912): F. Martin (Piano Quintet, 1920): J. Turina (Piano Quartet in A minor, Op. 67, 1931).

minor, and two piano quintets, both in C minor. The earlier of his
quintets, an attractive and relatively simple work, dated 1898, was
produced according to the composer 'under the impression made
on him by Brahms's death'; it remained unpublished, however,
and was not performed publicly until six years after Reger's own
death. The second quintet, dating from 1901 and published a year
later as his Op. 64, is altogether more complex. Typical of his so-
called 'savage period', it provides many tightly woven polyphonic
textures, in which themes, motifs, and counterthemes are em-
bedded within a restlessly chromatic harmonic scheme. Very striking in the first movement are the modifications applied to the
recapitulation, whereby certain four- and five-bar sections of the
original exposition material are simply omitted, and the resultant
severed ends (pitched a minor third lower) knitted neatly together
to provide the illusion at least of continuity. Leaner textures,
combined with a clearer treatment of tonality and counterpoint
which points forward towards the work of Hindemith, are evident
in Reger's two piano quartets, composed, respectively, nine and
thirteen years later. Noteworthy, in Op. 133 in A minor, are the
translucent textures of its scherzo, with muted strings sporting
elegantly, and often antiphonally, against a lightly patterned piano
part, and the notably Brahmsian thrust of its finale.

Based equally firmly in the Brahms tradition is the Piano Quintet
in C minor, Op. 1, by Dohnányi, composed in 1895 when he was
only seventeen years of age. Grandly rhetorical in style, the work
has four movements of which the lively scherzo, in A minor and
placed second, and the powerful rondo finale, which opens in 5/4
time, create the strongest impression. The piano part, reflecting
no doubt the young composer's outstanding keyboard skill, is
weighty and brilliant, but it is rarely allowed to subjugate the
strings, whose independent contributions are full of interest.
Greater refinement is evident, however, in the second of his
quintets, Op. 26 in E flat minor, which appeared nearly twenty
years later, in 1914. More lightly scored than its predecessor, with
an altogether more restrained piano part, it has three movements,
each of which begins and ends softly. Unusual in the opening
Allegro is the key-scheme of its recapitulation, where the first
subject, originally in E flat minor, returns in C minor, and the
charmingly chromatic second subject, previously centred around
G major/minor, returns in E (= F flat), in a Neapolitan relationship

to the basic tonic. Thematic recalls occur both in the middle movement, where the second subject of the previous Allegro provides a curious central episode to an elaborate set of variations on a waltz theme, and in the finale, where an accumulation of fugal complexities is gently countered, in the coda, by a return of the opening section of the whole work in its original simple setting.

Such nationalist elements as are evident in the first of the Dohnányi quintets reflect more the cosmopolitan 'Zigeuner' style of the period than any characteristics of genuinely Hungarian folk origin. At that time the era of research into the ethnic music of that part of Europe, in which Bartók and Kodály were to become so deeply involved, lay still in the future. However, in July 1904, at the end of what may be called his 'late-Romantic' period, Bartók, at the age of 23, completed a Piano Quintet in C, which, though written, on his own admission, under the influence of Dohnányi, shows some early signs of his growing interest in authentic folk music.[14] The young composer's inexperience is evident in the rambling structure of the work, the excess of climaxes, and the many unconvincing joins between sections; but the quintet reveals, none the less, powerful individuality, with its strongly-etched themes and rich harmonic resource. A degree of 'folk' colouring is provided in the first movement by the keyboard passages in imitation of a cimbalom, and in the slow movement by the *scordatura* tuning for both violins (with G strings temporarily lowered a semitone); but even more characteristically by the modal inflections found in many of the principal themes, and the graceful arabesques which repeatedly decorate the dotted-rhythm patterns of the slow movement (see Ex. 31). After the Quintet's first hearing in Vienna, in November 1904, the composer made a

Ex. 31. Bartók, Piano Quintet in C, slow movement

[14] D. Dille (ed.), Bartók, Piano Quintet in C (1903–4) (Editio Musica, Budapest, 1970).

number of cuts and revisions, and much later, in 1921, was persuaded, somewhat against his better judgement, to sanction a further performance. Its rapturous reception on this occasion may have afforded him some pleasure, though it is hardly likely to have been enhanced by a comment from a member of the audience, that he 'much preferred the quintet to some of his later music'.[15]

In 1907 the piano quintet again served as a medium for apprentice work by composers who were later to revolutionize the musical language, when Berg and Webern, both in their early twenties, and both engaged in study under Schoenberg, produced examples of the genre. Berg's Quintet, which is said to have been fugal in style, is unfortunately lost; but Webern's, a single movement in a broad sonata form, remains as a remarkable example of the late-Romantic German style.[16] In contrast to the somewhat undisciplined manner of the Bartók Quintet, this later work is as finely balanced in structure and scoring as it is restrained in expression, though underneath its controlled surface there lies evidence of a powerful nervous intensity of feeling. The stylistic debt to Wagner, Reger, and early Schoenberg is clear, but already there are signs of the passion for symmetry, the extreme distillation of thought, and the ear for delicate sonorities which were so greatly to characterize Webern's later work.[17]

Much broader in style is the Piano Quintet in C major, Op. 23, by Hans Pfitzner, which was composed a year later, in 1908.[18] A firm upholder of the German Romantic tradition, the composer appears in the work to be striving towards a special concept of beauty, as evidenced by the detailed expression indications he employs, such as that for the opening viola solo in the slow movement: 'Äusserst ruhig, mit tiefer Empfindung, aber bei aller Genauigkeit im Rhythmus gleichsam improvisierend vorzutragen' (extremely calm, with deep feeling, and although precise in rhythm, almost improvisatory in performance). In general, however, there is a curious instability of style, with grand Romantic gestures set in conjunction with ideas which are either banal or of

[15] Cited in the preface to D. Dille (ed.), Bartók, Piano Quintet in C.

[16] Jacques-Louis Monod (ed.), Webern, *Quintet für Streicher und Klavier* (Boelke-Bomart Edition, 12529, New York, 1974).

[17] D. Newlin, 'Anton von Webern: Quintet for String Quartet and Piano', *Notes*, x (1953), 674.

[18] See H. Truscott, 'The Importance of Hans Pfitzner: II—the Chamber Music', *Music-Survey* 1 (1947–9), 37.

apparently wilful obscurity. Most consistently sustained are the two central movements: a ternary-form Intermezzo with a finely scored opening for solo cello, ranging initially from G to e♭′′, before descending chromatically against pizzicato lower strings and staccato octaves on the piano; and an arch-shaped slow movement, of Mahlerian character, with an expressive funeral march for piano at its centre, accompanied by triplet 'drum-beats' on the strings. In vivid contrast is the mood provided by the finale; largely monothematic, and with much plain diatonic harmony, its markedly extrovert character is underlined by a moto perpetuo style in strong, march-like patterns. At the end, however, in place of the customary triumphal peroration, it dies down, reflectively, to a series of very soft repeated chords of C major.

For composers in more distant parts of Europe, German Romanticism, and the example of Brahms in particular, continued to provide a powerful source of inspiration. In England, Stanford, whose substantial output of chamber works includes two piano quartets and a piano quintet, was impelled towards a Germanic style at least partly by his early training with Reinecke in Leipzig and Kiel in Berlin. But however much rooted in central European practice, his music is also flavoured consistently by turns of phrase attributable to his native origins. In his D minor Piano Quintet, Op. 25, of 1886, dedicated 'To my friend Joseph Joachim', a charming juxtaposition of the competing spirits of Irish folk culture and German Romanticism is apparent between the Scherzo, a lively jig in 9/8 time, and the ensuing Andante, an expansive rondo, notable for its rich variety of ideas and finely crafted texture. Almost equally Germanic, though less obviously Brahmsian in character, is the Piano Quartet in E major (1906) by Sergey Taneyev who, despite his Russian origins and training, was deeply conservative in outlook and drawn more strongly towards central European traditions than to the nationalist trends cultivated by his contemporaries. The quartet provides strong evidence of the technical mastery for which he was renowned, partly in the vivid fugue at figure ⟨170⟩ and the ingenious combination of 'recalled' themes at ⟨209⟩ in the finale, but most strikingly in the elegant integration of adagio and scherzo sections in the central movement, a structure not unlike that found in the equivalent movements of Brahms's A major Violin Sonata, Op. 100, and Dvořák's E flat major String Quartet, Op. 51.

In France the intense focus on musical study in Paris, at the Conservatoire, the École Niedermeyer, and the Schola Cantorum, produced a large group of composers who, in succession to César Franck, were unusually closely interlinked as teachers and pupils, and were thus able to pass on characteristics of style and a superlative mastery of technique through successive generations. As in many French chamber works with piano of the period, the Piano Quartet in A major by Chausson and the quintets of Florent Schmitt and Vincent D'Indy each display a grandly 'symphonic' approach, skilfully tailored to the resources of the media. The Chausson quartet, his last completed chamber work, was composed between June and October 1897, two years before his early death, and reveals the new classical restraint he had developed by that time, in a reaction against earlier Wagnerian influence. The example of Franck is apparent in the colourful harmony, the restless modulations, and the theme transformations and recalls; but there is also a clarity of structure, an openness of texture, and a leaning towards modalism which lend the work an air of special distinction. Schmitt's Quintet (Op. 51 in B minor), which was completed in 1908 and dedicated to Fauré, is laid out on an even more massive scale, despite having only three movements. Prefacing each movement there is an extended introduction, containing a pair of ideas which establish the overall mood and recur later at significant points in the structure. The first of these, marked 'Lent et grave', and in common time, shows at once the influence of César Franck. After four initial bars of B minor chords, an impassioned descending theme on the strings is answered, at bar 21, by a gentle, pleading phrase for the piano, marked 'p expressif, un peu plus lent', in a manner which recalls, irresistibly, the opening of the earlier composer's quintet (see Ex. 32).

Similarly, the spirit of Fauré can be felt behind the introduction to the slow movement, where, following a solo for muted viola, the piano, in a section marked 'Comme les cloches au loin', provides B♭ octaves against a background of rustling tremolandi on muted strings. In this case the example lurking in the composer's mind, though more in general concept than precise detail, is evidently the 'Bells of Cadirac' section at the beginning of the slow movement of Fauré's Second Piano Quartet (see p. 81).

In all three movements there is an abundance of well-contrasted themes, the eloquence of which results more from the richness of

Ex. 32
Schmitt, Piano Quintet in B minor, Op. 51, 1st movement

Franck, Piano Quintet in F minor, 1st movement

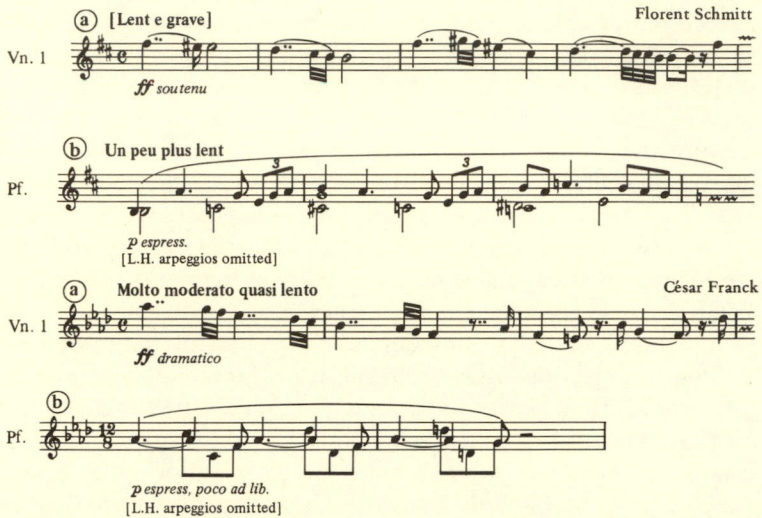

their supporting, Wagnerian, harmony and vividly varied scoring, than from any intrinsic melodic distinction. However, as 'leitmotifs' for recall in the last movement, they contribute to a cyclic pattern of the most elaborate type. In common with the preceding movements the finale has an introduction centred around two main ideas, the first of which involves a quaint (and perhaps not entirely necessary) modulation back from D flat major, the key of the slow movement, to B minor, the home tonic, and the second, in 8/4 time, a prominent duet for cello and viola. At bar 26 (figure 5), the first subject proper appears, 'une folle et sauvage danse' in 5/4 time, but marked by Schmitt 'Pas trop vite, encore qu'ardent et joyeux'; and this, together with a more lyrical second subject (which is said to be derived from the second subject of the first movement, though the connection is not very obvious) completes the range of significant new material. Following a reprise of the first subject proper, at 19, theme 2 from the introduction of the first movement reappears on the second violin against a simple triplet accompaniment, as the first of an extended sequence of cyclic returns. Then, in the words of the composer, 'after a last repetition of the main theme [of the movement] in its original key of B (major and minor mixed), all the principal themes are gathered together in a melée: the first subject of the first movement, augmented, the first of the third movement, augmented and diminished, the incidental theme of the first movement, and the first theme of the introduction to the first movement. The finale is concluded *fff* with the theme of the dance in ever-increasing animation.'[19]

More temperate in style, though equally adroit technically, is the four-movement Piano Quintet in G minor, Op. 81, by Franck's pupil, Vincent D'Indy, which appeared in 1924, the year of Fauré's death. By that later date, on the evidence of D'Indy's work, the cultivation of immensely repetitive cyclic structures appears to have lost some of its former appeal. Only at one place, in the coda to the finale, is there a clear instance of thematic recall, where the second theme of the slow movement returns climactically, at a slow tempo in a fast context, very much in the way that the 'motto' theme is reintroduced at the end of the finale in Franck's quintet. Elsewhere, a unifying link, evident more to the eye than the ear, is provided by a tiny four-note pattern which appears initially on the first violin in bars 4 and 5 of the first movement, as the final notes of the opening phrase of its principal theme. Subsequently, it contributes to the development and coda of the first movement; forms part of the main theme of the slow movement; and appears at the start of the second subject in the finale. But in none of these contexts is it sufficiently memorable to make much of an impact. Most consistently effective is the second movement of the work, a scherzo and trio in D minor, which alone remains free of the persistent four-note pattern. Both sections are in 5/4 time, with varied 2 + 3 and 3 + 2 accentuation in the scherzo underlining lively exchanges between the strings and piano.

A late reminder of the ancient regime in an era of change and revolution, D'Indy's quintet, for all its merits, reveals a romantic ripeness of style which, by 1924, had already turned largely to decay. However, in what may be regarded as a transitional period during the first two decades of the century, the quartet and quintet

---

[19] It is indicative of the exaggerated importance which Schmitt appears to have attached to his system of thematic recall that he should have felt impelled to describe it in such detail in his preface to the published score.

genres, though almost entirely ignored (*pace* the youthful essays of Bartók, Berg, and Webern) by the first generation of radical innovators, retained sufficient of the force generated earlier, particularly by Brahms and his followers, to provide for a continuing process of development. Although working within relatively restricted boundaries of style, the composers involved contributed profusely to the repertoire; and in many cases with works which are not only of major proportions, but also lack nothing in the way of vigorous ideas and powerfully effective means of expression.

5
Transition and Change

WHILE the closely knit group of César Franck's successors (not only Schmitt and D'Indy, but also Pierné, Vierne, Roger-Ducasse, and others) continued, during the first decades of the new century, to exploit the 'symphonic' type of piano quintet, with its peculiar emphasis on thematic unification and extreme richness of texture, Fauré, with his two contributions to the genre—Op. 89 in D minor and Op. 115 in C minor—pursued an altogether more independent line, in which purity of style and classical poise were the distinguishing traits. Enlarging on the highly personal musical language created during his first period, not least with his piano quartets, he provided in these works of his maturity a new intensity of vision, unfailingly emotional, but couched always in terms of moderation and restraint. Eugene Ysaÿe, who, with his quartet and Fauré as pianist, gave the first performance of Op. 89, in Brussels in 1906, precisely described the essential nature of the composer's thought when he referred to his 'total rejection of showmanship' and his ability to create 'absolute music in the purest sense of the words'.

The lengthy gestation period which preceded the completion of Fauré's First Piano Quintet in 1905 has been traced in interesting detail by Robert Orledge in his distinguished study of the composer's life and work.[1] The first idea for the work appeared in a sketchbook entry of 1887, where an outline of the main theme of the finale, in F major and in 2/4 time, was included amongst drafts of the 'Pie Jesu' from the *Requiem* and the song 'Clair de lune'. At this stage the composer's declared intention was to compose a third piano quartet; it was not until four years later that expansion to a quintet was finally decided upon. Subsequently, progress was slow and painful (as is made clear in a letter of August, 1904, in which the composer refers to the work as 'this animal of a quintet'), and undertaken between periods of concentration on

[1] R. Orledge, *Gabriel Fauré* (London, 1979), 106–9.

other compositions.[2] Particular difficulty appears to have been caused by the development section of the first movement and the ending of the slow movement, each of which in fact provide in their final form impressive evidence of the continuing precision of the composer's musical judgement.

The first movement is overridingly melodic, even song-like, in character, but with a sustained dynamism created by its rich harmonic colouring and inventive piano writing. Often seemingly improvisatory in style, its craftsmanship is none the less impeccable and the controlling mind behind its structure entirely sure. The opening, which differs in virtually every important respect from the pithy subject statements of the Austro–German sonata tradition, comprises a 29-bar paragraph in a modal D minor, part Dorian, part transposed Aeolian (Ex. 33a), with the strings singing in smooth lines against rippling arpeggios in demi-semiquavers high on the piano, outlining a gently shifting pattern of harmonies. At bar 30, in immediate contrast, the strings alone, at their lowest pitch, provide a vigorous rhythmic motif (Ex. 33b), still in D minor, which, together with a strongly etched, single-bar phrase (Ex. 33c), given first on the piano at bar 43, features prominently in later developments. After a moment of repose in F major, the development section is launched at bar 68 with a new theme, initially on the second violin, which carries the music forward by combining freely and elegantly with various forms of the opening theme (see Ex. 33d).

The central slow movement, in G major, has a basic binary structure—ABA′B′Coda—made complex by the process of continuous development which it embraces. Contrast is created between the ethereal opening idea, with its limping, off-beat phrases on the strings, and the more 'concrete' second section (in B minor), the main theme of which is shadowed continually by another part in canon at a crotchet's distance. As so often in Fauré, it is the apparently self-effacing accompaniments which play a major part in defining the mood and controlling the structure. At the first appearance of the B section, for example, the persistent triplet quavers of the opening give way to quadruplet semiquavers to provide, increasingly, a sense of underlying disquiet. But subse-

---

[2] G. Fauré, *Lettres intimes* (1885–1924), ed. Philippe Fauré-Fremiet (Paris, 1951), 88.

Ex. 33. Fauré, Piano Quintet in D minor, Op. 89, 1st movement

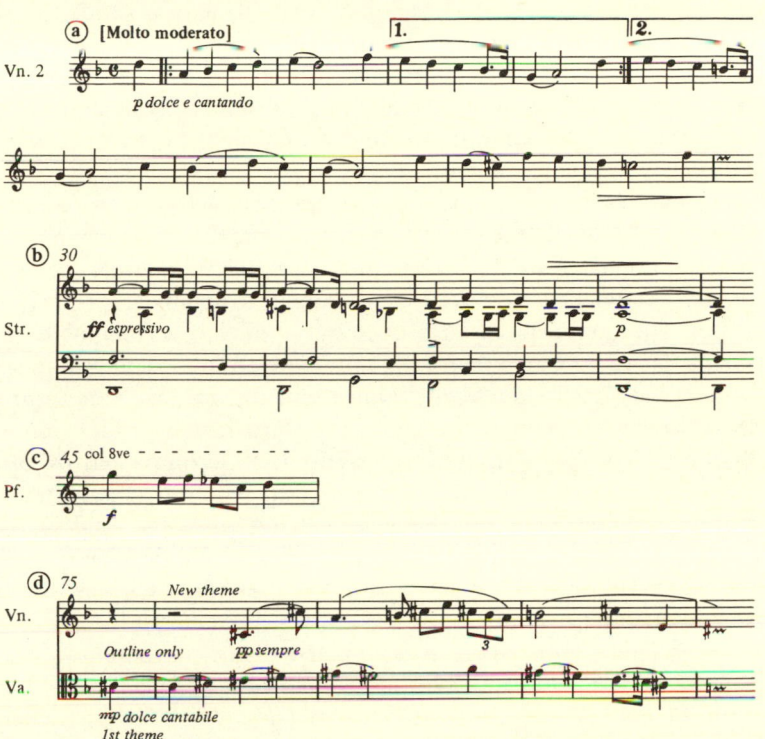

quently, as the two main themes interconnect, their supporting patterns are varied or exchanged, to move purposefully out of step with their original partners. A striking example is provided by the heavily-disguised point of recapitulation, at the fourth bar after figure ⑪. Arriving at the end of a gradual crescendo, through a typical extended sequential passage based on fragments of both main ideas, the original theme of A is allotted, fortissimo, to the second violin and cello, its mood greatly transformed, not only by entirely new harmony but also by a continuing background of quadruplet semiquavers. Not until the fifth bar of theme, after a diminuendo, are the triplet patterns and barcarolle-style accompaniment of the opening restored, together with their associated sense of calm. The final bars of the movement which, as we have seen earlier, created particular problems for the composer, are as finely crafted as any in his output. Preceded once again by an extended sequence, based on a more rugged version of the first theme, the home key of G major is reached, with a sudden *p*, at figure ⑱; and against a background of faltering semiquavers on the piano, an even more expressive version of the B theme on the second violin sinks towards a close, coloured, typically, by a harmonic side-step to F major and a final approach to the tonic through a secondary seventh on the major submediant.

Apparently to counterbalance the inwardness of expression and rhythmic fluidity of the preceding movement, the finale begins in a bright D major, with a four-square, marching pattern on the piano—derived, as we have already noted, from an early sketch of 1887. The structure of this opening is unusually inflexible for Fauré. Three 24-bar paragraphs are involved, each containing six ostinato phrases in identical rhythm, four of them in D major and the other two, interspersed and set a third lower, with E minor harmony. Following its initial presentation, accompanied by pizzicato strings, the ostinato, in the second paragraph, supports a hymnic countertheme for the whole string ensemble, and in the third, underpins a delicate pattern in quavers for the piano, with the hands two octaves apart. Thereafter the strait-jacket is loosed and a process of almost continuous development ensues, varied only at figure ⑩, where a secondary theme, in B minor with leaping octaves, is introduced. In general the movement is handled with the composer's customary inventiveness; but it never entirely frees itself from the restricted premises from which it begins. At the work's rather unsatisfactory first performance in 1906, Fauré is said to have expressed concern that the similarity he had created between the main theme of his finale and the 'Ode to Joy' melody from Beethoven's Choral Symphony was too obvious. Certainly there is some resemblance between the themes, but it is hardly excessive. More probably the deeper, unexpressed, cause of his unease was the unyielding nature of his principal idea and the somewhat over-conventional ending to the work he had provided.

Completed some fifteen years later, in 1921, the Second Piano Quintet differs structurally from its predecessor mainly by its inclusion of a scherzo. The lack of such a movement in the earlier work is said to have disappointed its original audiences, a situation the composer may well have wished to rectify. But in doing so he moved a little surprisingly against the three-movement pattern (with a central slow movement) found in all his other third-period chamber works. In the quintet, the added scherzo (in E flat major) is a miracle of quicksilver pliancy, which in lightness and *élan* surpasses even the corresponding movements in the piano quartets. Notable features include the first violin's graceful countertheme, with simple cross-phrasing, entered against the principal subject's darting semiquavers on the piano at bar 35 (see Ex. 34); the vivid

Ex. 34. Fauré, Piano Quintet in C minor, Op. 115, 2nd movement

chromatic descent for the strings in repeated semiquaver chords against the piano's scales at bar 95, resumed five bars later with the roles reversed; and, at figure ⑩, the 'false' recapitulation, pitched a major seventh lower, as if, momentarily, in E (= F flat) major.

Apart from the inclusion of this extra movement, the overall structure of the Second Quintet matches that of its predecessor quite closely. As in the earlier work the first movement adopts a process of continuous development, in which recurrences of the principal theme and its accompaniment (at bars 83, 177, and 267), herald the start of new sections, simply as stabilizing moments of recall rather than any more conventional form of recapitulation. Other points of similarity between the movements include the arpeggio patterns of their opening piano accompaniments, the intense subsidiary themes for the strings alone (at bars 30 and 35 respectively), and the frequent combination of motifs as a developmental manœuvre. Both movements end in the major, but with a powerful, perhaps somewhat over-extended, affirmation of C major in the case of the Second Quintet, in contrast to the mood of calm contemplation found at the equivalent place in the first.

The slow movement of the later quintet corresponds to its predecessor in its general expressive character and key (G major), the latter necessarily with a simpler relationship to the central tonic—the major dominant as compared to the more modally orientated major subdominant of the D minor work. But in place of the plain binary structure of the earlier movement, there is a rondo-like pattern, with spaced recurrences of the initial, intensely chromatic, theme-complex, each heralding the start of additional, but shorter, sections. At bar 27 contrast is provided by a simple second theme, in a modal E minor, parts of which are later skilfully woven into the 'rondo' returns to establish a closely integrated texture.

For the finale, Fauré again adopts an underlying ostinato pattern, but one very different from that in the First Quintet. In place of the lengthy, march-like theme used in the earlier movement, its successor involves only a short bass figure in repeated 'hemiola' cross-rhythms, which, by inserting a tie across the barline and a crotchet rest at the start of bar 3, make four bars of 3/4 time sound like two bars of 3/2 time. And this, in the minor mode and maintained for only 38 bars, serves as the accompaniment to a scherzo-like theme, presented initially by the viola and second violin in turn. Noteworthy, by comparison with the First Quintet, is the lightness of the piano writing, both in this movement and the previous one, much of which comprises two strands only. Furthermore there are surprisingly few places where the left hand of the piano part contributes thematically to the texture; bars 35–42 of the slow movement provide a rare exception.

At its resoundingly successful first performance, in May 1921, the Second Quintet was received with the greatest admiration, and not a little astonishment. As a critic of the occasion observed 'We knew well that Gabriel Fauré had remarkable talent, but not that his music had attained such heights. The more we heard of the work, the greater was the enthusiasm; but it was an enthusiasm touched with remorse that we had perhaps misjudged the old man who held such a gift in his hands.'[3]

During the decade preceding the composition of Fauré's Second Quintet, important contributions were made to the repertoire, both of piano quartets and quintets, by a substantial group of British composers, including Frank Bridge, Bax, Howells, Elgar, and Walton, between whom, despite their differences in age and background, various links can be traced. Bridge and Howells, for instance, were both pupils of Stanford at the Royal College of Music, and their music shares a clarity of expression and refinement of technique which reflect his teaching. Bridge, the elder by seven years, provides in his *Phantasy Quartet* in F sharp minor (1910) a relatively conventional melodic and harmonic style drawn, largely through Stanford's example, from Brahms. It was not until after the war, initially with his Piano Sonata of 1924, that, under the influence of Schoenberg, Berg, and Bartók, his work gained the more powerfully 'modernist' image for which it was later acclaimed. In his quartet he exploits, with superior judgement, the type of structure fostered by the prize competitions of W. W. Cobbett, in which the principal features of a three- or four-movement work are compressed into a single movement, with much use of thematic transformation and spaced reprises. Howells, on the other hand, reflects in his the finely-wrought A minor Quartet (a three-movement work written in 1916 when he was 24) the burgeoning English pastoral style of the time, with modal writing and a use of folksong idioms, related to the work of Holst, Warlock, and, particularly, Vaughan Williams.[4]

Links are evident also between Howells and Walton (whose four-movement Quartet in D minor, including a scherzo, was completed in 1919 when he was barely seventeen), not only as the youngest composers of the group, but also because their styles, at

---

[3] R. Orledge, *Gabriel Fauré*, 182.

[4] The Piano Quartet bears the dedication 'To the Hill at Chosen and Ivor Gurney who knows it'. In a letter to Howells from the Western Front, of 24 Aug. 1916, Gurney wrote, 'It is hard lines not to be able to hear my Quartett, for Miss Scott [Marion Scott] is the author of the good news that it is your Best Work.' R. K. R. Thornton, *Ivor Gurney: Collected Letters* (Manchester, 1991), 135.

this stage in their careers, enjoyed a largely common basis, rooted in the English traditions of the time.[5] Shared characteristics include modal and pentatonic melodic writing, an emphasis on cyclic recall between movements, and a command of apt theme combination—for example, in Howells's first movement, at nine bars after figure ⑩, where part of the opening theme, on the piano, is set against the second subject, on the strings; and in Walton's, from bar 119, where the first and second subjects form a contrapuntal 'pair' on violin and cello, respectively. Another common feature, noticeable particularly in the slow movements, is a romantic richness of harmony, of a type introduced into English music (largely from French models) by John Ireland, whose work was then gaining increasing recognition. Specific examples are, in Howells, the imaginative lead-back to the return of the principal theme in the slow movement, between figures ㉖ and ㉙, and, in Walton, the warmly expressive opening bars of the third movement (see Ex. 35). There are however pointers also towards a later divergence in style, not only in Walton's sharper harmonies and greater rhythmic *élan*, which contrast markedly with Howells' quieter, more meditative manner, but also in the emphatic character of his piano writing, which, even after the 'slimming' process undertaken with the composer's assent by Robert Kinloch Anderson (which led to the publication of a revised edition, in 1976), exceeds in vigour and chordal richness—and by no means always with advantage to the balance of the ensemble—anything found in the work of his older contemporary.

Links between Bax and Elgar are less readily established, although, with their primarily orchestral orientation, it is not surprising that each contributed piano quintets in the grand 'symphonic' style of the period. Typically rhapsodical in manner, with sweeping melodic gestures and a rich harmonic palette, Bax's very lengthy G minor Quintet, of 1915, opens with a grand sonata movement, based on three principal themes which aptly characterize different aspects of his musical personality. The first, on the cello, and supported by semiquaver arpeggio figuration on the piano, has a bold upward thrust which with varied rhythmic detail expresses freedom and challenge, somewhat in the spirit of his

[5] See F. Howes, 'Pianoforte Quartet' in *The Music of William Walton*, Vol. 1, 10 (London, 1942; 2nd edn., 1973).

Ex. 35. Walton, Piano Quartet in D minor, 3rd movement

tone poem, *Tintagel*, of 1917; while the second, a motif of narrow range in C major marked 'not humorous, very rhythmical', conveys the impression of an Irish dance, while contriving also to recall, distantly, part of the opening of Sibelius's Third Symphony. And the last, the true second subject in the distant key of E major, is a broadly pentatonic 'folk' theme, with gently circling repetitions around a central tonic (see Ex. 36*a*, *b*, and *c*).

The expressive scheme of the slow movement (possibly following some hidden 'programme') hinges largely on the contrast between its warmly romantic opening melody, scored initially for piano against pizzicato strings, and some quiet passages in four-part

Ex. 36. Bax, Piano Quintet in G minor, 1st movement

harmony on the strings, marked 'pianissimo: cold and unemotional', and each punctuated by bare chords on the piano. Both ideas return, the modal theme in grandiose style after letter $\boxed{C}$, and the 'cold' patterns to form a subdued, rather sombre, ending. For his finale, the composer reverts to the principal subject matter of the first movement and, turning to the major mode, recasts it so thoroughly that the effect is not so much of 'theme transference' as of 'movement transference'. Towards the end, a 'Lento con gran espressione' section, featuring the themes of both Ex. 36*a* and *c* from the first movement, provides an impressive climax, during which the minor mode is finally restored.

Elgar's A minor Piano Quintet, inscribed 'Brinkwells, 1918', is the last in the short series of chamber works, including a violin sonata and a string quartet, both in E minor, which he completed at the end of the First World War. Although he had produced in his youth some light pieces for chamber resources, these late works were his only compositions of the type of classical proportions, and represent, for a predominantly orchestral and choral composer, a curious end-of-career change of direction, the nearest parallel to which is probably Debussy's sudden return to chamber composition in 1915, three years before his death.

Immediately striking (and indeed disconcerting to some of Elgar's contemporaries) is the mysterious introduction to the first movement, with its muttering rhythms on the strings, set against a solemn melody in octaves on the piano. It was apparently in reference to this that, in a letter to Ernest Newman, the dedicatee of the work, the composer wrote, 'It's strange music, I think, and I like it—but—it's ghostly stuff'.[6] The word 'ghostly', referred apparently to an underlying tale about some dead trees at Bedham Copse, not far from the composer's cottage, 'Brinkwells', near Fittleworth in Sussex. These, according to what was alleged to be a local legend, were the remains of a group of Spanish monks (somewhat strangely domiciled, in earlier days, in the English countryside) who had been struck down for dabbling in black magic. Sadly, however, recent investigations have revealed no trace of any such legend at Fittleworth, nor indeed of any settlement there of monks, Spanish or otherwise.[7] As a later embellishment of the story, an attempt has been made to identify the start of the piano part as a reference to the eleventh-century plainsong antiphon, 'Salve Regina', a not implausible idea in view of the supposed legendary 'programme', though the quotation, if it is one, is very brief. From a purely musical point of view it is the contrast between the sinister-sounding introduction and the vigorous, decidedly Brahmsian, Allegro which ensues that has tended to cause puzzlement. Bernard Shaw, who attended a private performance of the work early in 1919, found difficulty in reconciling the mysteries of the opening with the formal, rather weak, fugato at figure ⑩ of the first movement. 'You cannot begin a movement in such a magical way . . . and then suddenly relapse into the expected', he wrote to the composer in March 1919.[8] But, setting aside the question of 'academic fugatos', there are distinguished precedents for the conjunction of a mysterious introduction with a plain-spoken Allegro—the opening of Mozart's 'Dissonance' Quartet in C, K. 465, for instance. More important, however, is the extent to which Elgar's introduction serves to integrate the movement as a whole; and in this respect there are both gains and losses. On the credit side there is the unifying effect produced by recurrences of parts of the introduction during the main Allegro; and its return, in substance, as an epilogue. But against that must be set the many whimsical changes of mood and tempo which are necessarily created, and the somewhat piecemeal structure which results.

In both the second and third movements, thematic recall, which

---

[6] See M. Kennedy, *Portrait of Elgar* (London, 1968; 3rd edn., 1987), 276.

[7] See M. Pope, introduction to the miniature score of the Quintet, Eulenburg No. 399, for a detailed survey of the factual background to the work's creation.

[8] M. Kennedy, *Portrait of Elgar*, 279.

draws on ideas from the first movement, and from its 'ghostly' introduction in particular, provides an effective means of integration. A notable example in the finale is the eerie section which precedes the recapitulation (from three bars before 55), where, in addition to ideas from the introduction, a shadowy outline of the second subject of the first Allegro (originally at figure ⑥) returns. Also very striking is the way in which the plaintive opening of the finale, a recall of the second main idea of the original 'ghostly' introduction, is abruptly set aside after only ten bars by a vivid accelerando lead, over a dominant seventh, to the ensuing Allegro, as if to exorcise (though, as it transpires, not entirely successfully) its former unearthly connotations.

The Piano Quintet is often claimed as the grandest in scale and richness of ideas of Elgar's chamber works, and there is certainly an impressive sweep about much of the writing, particularly in the exciting manner in which the various climaxes are approached. However, in all three movements, the impression of size results more from an excess of repetition, both exact and sequential, than from any intrinsic largeness of concept. The work's basic chamber orientation is unmistakable; but it is hard not to conclude that at times the composer may have been lured into an orchestral mode of thought, with an imagined variety of scoring and instrumental colour to justify the many repeats.

Following the brief 'Indian summer' of Romanticism represented by these British works, and by those of French origin discussed earlier, the cultivation of the piano quartet and quintet declined for some considerable time. The possibility of further progress in purely traditionalist terms appears to have been regarded as limited in the post-war era; and attempts at a more innovative approach were discouraged, at least temporarily, by the largely conservative image which the genres had acquired. As a result the major developments of the first half of the century—from Impressionism and jazz to atonality and serialism—made virtually no immediate impact. However, two exceptions from the early 1920s deserve special attention: the First Piano Quintet, Op. 80, of Charles Koechlin, written mainly between 1917 and 1921,[9] and the First Quintet, Op. 33, by Ernest Bloch of 1923, each of which dis-

---

[9] Ch. Koechlin, *Quintette pour Piano et Instruments à Cordes* (Editions Max Eschig, Paris, 1985).

play, in their very different ways, uncompromisingly modernist approaches.

The Koechlin quintet provides what is surely a unique attempt to convey, in purely instrumental terms, the sufferings of a soldier in the trenches during the Great War, an attempt made all the more remarkable by the fact that the composer, because of his impaired health (from tuberculosis contracted during the 1880s), lacked any actual experience of soldiering. In the ordinary way it seems natural to assume that abstract music, the 'innocent' art, if it is to retain probity, lacks the ability to evoke the horrors of war in a realistic fashion—a function more aptly achieved in literary or pictorial terms. Yet, in his monumental four-movement quintet, Koechlin not only creates a vividly realistic effect, using an ultra-modern dissonant style, but also achieves a firmly controlled musical structure, in which a sense of unity is provided by thematic development and metamorphosis, and the spaced reprise of ideas.[10] In the manner of a symphonic poem, the work traces through its four movements: a period of anxious waiting for what is to come ('L'attente obscure de ce qui sera . . .'); an attack by the enemy, and wounding ('L'assaut de l'ennemi . . . la blessure'); the solace of Nature ('La Nature consolatrice . . .'); and an expression of joy at escape from the earlier terrors ('Final: La joie . . .'). Although only the bare outline of a programme is given, the impression consistently created by the music is of an individual's personal reaction to events, rather than a purely generalized description.

The opening Andante arouses a sense of fearful anticipation by the use of chromatic scales on muted strings, low in pitch and very soft in dynamics, against which the piano provides fourth- and fifth-based chords and a succession of arched counterthemes in quavers. In the second movement, which fulfils the role, conventionally, of a scherzo, there are two principal ideas, stated initially by strings and piano in succession, which take on, progressively, a rich variety of shapes—augmented, inverted, fragmented, and so on—but never return in precisely their original forms. The underlying harmony relies to a large extent on bitonality, a favourite technique of Koechlin's, but one which he uses more as a means of

[10] See R. Orledge, *Charles Koechlin (1867–1950): His Life and Works* (London, 1989), 121.

underlining expressive detail than as a doctrinaire system. A two-bar passage from figure ⑳ shows a short-scale instance of his methods. While the right hand of the piano part contributes plain chords of E flat, D flat, F, and E flat minor, which agree well enough with the violin lines (provided enharmonic equivalents are taken for their sharpened notes), the remaining elements—piano left hand, viola, and cello—outline chord patterns in conflicting keys on each successive dotted crotchet beat (see Ex. 37). The

Ex. 37. Koechlin, Piano Quintet, Op. 80, 2nd movement

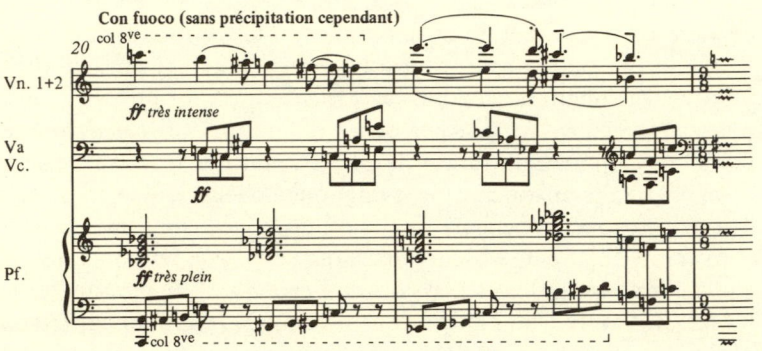

procedure, which is employed more persistently in this tension-ridden movement than elsewhere in the work, can only be interpreted as symbolic of the hand-to-hand fighting between the warring sides.

The remaining movements, following the expressive plan of the work, show a gradual easing of the level of dissonance, a more varied melodic style, and a greater leaning towards tonality. In the finale a key signature is used for the first time (that of A major), and with the subsequent addition of two further sharps, B is established finally as the home key, but with no third to determine its mode. In some respects the last movement is the most overtly pictorial of all. At the opening, with the clear intention of depicting joy in a religious context, a representation of pealing bells on the piano alternates with a string section in a mock-Renaissance church style, with 'voices' in imitation presenting a solemn theme in minim and crotchet notation. Then at figure ⑦ a new Allegro section, marked 'joyeux, lumineux, doux', provides freer, more varied melodic patterns over simpler harmony, initially centred on

E major. Towards the end both the 'church polyphony' section and the bells motif return, and combine with the 'joyeux' Allegro themes to form some wonderfully expansive final paragraphs.

This remarkable composition by Koechlin is unique in the vividness of its portrayal of the experience of war. There are, however, two other works, less intensely associated with war, which may briefly be mentioned: the Piano Quintet, Op. 42, of 1919 by the south German composer, Hermann Zilcher (1881–1948), and the Piano Quintet in G, dated 1926, by Franz Schmidt (1874–1939). The former, though lacking any great individuality, aims, by its incorporation of appropriate song and hymn melodies, to provide a similar condemnation of the horrors of the First World War; and the latter is one of the many works—including concertos by Ravel, Prokofiev, and Britten (*Diversions on a Theme*, 1940, rev. 1954), which were written for the pianist Paul Wittgenstein (brother of the philosopher), who lost his right arm in the Great War. Fluent and attractive in style, the work owes much to the central German tradition of Brahms, Strauss, and Reger, with some evidence, also, of the influence of Hindemith. The left-handed keyboard part is complex and wide-ranging and, with a minimum amount of doubling, blends gracefully with the strings. The need, however, for the piano to assert itself frequently through high pitched passages means that the cello is forced to provide an unusually large amount of the bass for the whole ensemble.

Less extreme in style than the Koechlin work, but also markedly innovative for its time, is the Piano Quintet in C by Ernest Bloch, his first essay in the form, which was completed in 1923, a year before his naturalization as a US citizen, when he was teaching at the Institute of Music in Cleveland, Ohio. A large-scale work in three movements, it is typically eclectic in manner, with stylistic debts not only to various leading composers of the period, but also to elements drawn from Bloch's national and cultural heritage, all assimilated into an entirely personal and individual musical language.[11] Amongst contemporary composers, those who, in general terms, exerted the clearest influence are Stravinsky, for subtleties of rhythm and the structural use of ostinatos; Hindemith,

---

[11] For a discussion of Bloch's national and racial traits, and an analysis of his First Piano Quintet, see Dika Newlin, 'The Later Works of Ernest Bloch', *The Musical Quarterly*, 33 (1947), 443.

for the use of expanded tonal harmony; Bartók, for a folk-style directness of expression and a 'fauvist' exploitation of tone-colour; and in the slow movement of the Quintet in particular, Ravel, for refinement of scoring and localized moments of harmonic piquancy. At the same time, overriding other considerations, there is Bloch's deep immersion in Jewish culture, derived from his home environment in Switzerland, and in particular from his grandfather, who was president of the Jewish community of Lengau in the canton of Aargau. In a number of his works, notably those of his so-called Jewish Cycle (1911–18), such as *Schelomo— Rapsodie Hebraïque* (1916), the *Israel* Symphony (1912–16), and the *Trois Poèmes Juifs* (1918), direct quotations and motivic references are made to Jewish chant; but in other instances, especially in his classically designed instrumental chamber works, the connection is established through features of a more generalized Jewish character, such as melodic forms which are inflected by augmented seconds and fourths, solo writing in an emotive rhapsodic style, irregular phrasing, repeated changes of metre, and the occasional use of 'snap' rhythms. His employment of quartertones in his First Piano Quintet and various other works coincided almost exactly with the first major experiment made in that direction by Alois Hába, in his Third String Quartet; and this technique, in turn, provides a quasi-oriental flavour which is readily relatable to Jewish cantillation.

In structure, the First Quintet is dependent largely upon a closely-wrought cyclic system, whereby much of the thematic material in each movement is derived from two motto ideas of contrasted character, one tightly spaced and the other wide ranging, which are announced at the start, during an 18-bar introduction. The first 'motto' (see Ex. 38a) occurs low on the piano in long note-values to give the simple pattern of a descending minor third and a descending minor second, each of which returns to the tonic C. Against this the strings provide an accompaniment in triplet quaver groups, each with its central note sharpened by a quartertone. Though startling enough to the eye the effect of this is considerably less so to the ear, since the speed of the triplet groups negates almost entirely any microtonal pitch distinction. What remains most clearly audible is the upward movement, and back, of a semitone and a minor third, providing a half-concealed inversion and reversal of the initial motto pattern, sounding below.

Ex. 38. Bloch, Piano Quintet No. 1
(a) 1st movement
(b) 1st movement
(c) 2nd movement
(d) 3rd movement
(e) 1st movement
(f) Piano Quintet No. 2, 1st movement

The second, wide-ranging, 'motto' (see Ex. 38b) enters on the piano in bar 6, and provides the basic intervals of the fourth, perfect and augmented, and the major seventh which, in subsequent transformations, are to shape the first subject of the movement and determine thereafter much of its thematic and harmonic detail. Throughout the remainder of the work, the two 'mottos' make repeated interventions, most obviously as the principal subjects of the second and third movements (see Ex. 38c and d) and in the final bars of the first movement, where their basic profiles—wide-ranging and tightly-spaced—are thrown together in a vividly dramatic juxtaposition (see Ex. 38e).

Strong contrasts of mood and dynamics are a common feature of Bloch's writing, not only between movements but also between individual sections. A striking instance, in the first movement, is the passage which links the first subject group to the second; after rising to an exceptionally loud climax the music appears to exhaust itself, and, at bar 66, sinks back rapidly to a murmur, for the viola's entry with the second theme. Equally impressive, at this point, is the sudden change of mood which occurs, between the strong forward drive of the first group and the static, delicately impressionist character of the second, with its melancholy, 'oriental', fragments on individual strings (again featuring quartertones) set against a pianissimo, two-note tremolando on the piano. The procedure is worked out in its most elaborate, and indeed most touchingly beautiful, form in the finale, where the many conflicts inherent in the powerfully Bartókian style of the music are resolved, from figure ⑤⓪, in a coda of wonderful tenderness.[12] Marked, characteristically, 'molto calmo' it proceeds through some translucent harmonies, involving parallel triads over a tonic pedal bass, to the plainest of final cadences in C major.

The magical effect which 'calm after the storm' can provide as an ending is one which Bloch seems particularly to have favoured. Further noteworthy examples are to be found in the finales of both his Second String Quartet (1946) and his Second Piano Quintet. This later work, which was completed in 1957, two years before his death, while he was living in retirement in Oregon, is shorter and more tightly concentrated than its predecessor. But, despite the gap of thirty years which separates them, the two compositions have much in common, not only in their overall, three-movement, structures and shared 'calmo' endings, but also in various specific thematic shapes. At figure ③ in the first movement, for example, the powerful subsidiary theme on the first violin—a complete twelve-note pattern, plus two additional notes—relates plainly to the second 'motto' of the First Quintet, expanding its leaping fourths to fifths, but retaining its characteristic falling tritone (see Ex. 38f). The two outer movements, both unequivocally in E minor/major, are brusque and unsentimental, and involve a surprisingly large amount of exact doubling between the piano and strings. Sharply-etched motifs, often upward-leaping and underlined by sforzato accents, characterize the first movement, while the finale, once again fiercely Bartókian in style, includes not only passages in a drumming, peasant-dance manner, at figure ③③, but also full-blooded, though short-lived,

---

[12] See J. Chissell, 'Style in Bloch's Chamber Music', *Music and Letters*, 24 (1943), 30, for a discussion of the contributory influences on Bloch's writing.

fugatos, initially at figure ㉕ and again at three bars after ㊵. As in the previous work, a subtle recall of motifs provides a link between all three movements, but there is no firmly organized set of 'motto' themes. And once again the slow movement stands apart in its quietly meditative manner, its principal melodic intervals contracted to semitones. The leading idea, a motif of four notes, c′′, b′, f′′, e′′, is threaded into a sustained texture, somewhat in the manner of a fugue subject, and creates overall the effect of an extended pattern of variations.

During the intervening years between the two works by Bloch, there appeared piano quartets and quintets by a number of composers who, like Bloch himself, had connections both with Paris and with some location in the United States. Amongst them were three Americans, Aaron Copland, Walter Piston, and Roy Harris, each of whom had studied in Paris during the 1920s with Nadia Boulanger; and, on the European side, Bohuslav Martinů, the prolific Czech composer, who had worked in Paris with Roussel from 1923, and in 1941 moved to the United States, where he undertook teaching and advisory work and, for three years, held the professorship of composition at Princeton.

Martinů's sizeable contribution to the repertoire comprises three piano quintets and two piano quartets. The earliest of the quintets (No. 'O'), a student work completed in 1911 when the composer, at the age of 21, had just completed his studies with Josef Suk at the Prague Conservatoire, is of historical interest only. Much later, there appeared in Paris his important first quintet, which was published in 1933, and this was succeeded by a further one, in 1944, after the composer's move to the United States. The first piano quartet was also written in America, in 1942, and was partnered five years later by a shorter, more lightweight, work for the less orthodox combination of piano, oboe, violin, and cello.

In style these compositions display a remarkable compound of inherent and acquired traits. The inherent features derive from the composer's Czech roots, and in particular from his interest in Moravian folksong. Although he rarely uses actual folk-melodies (and then mainly in his songs and shorter choral works), their general style—including narrowness of compass, repetition of motifs, and pentatonic colouring—shapes the melodic character of much of his instrumental writing. But overlaying this basic simplicity of manner there are modernist traits which the composer acquired during his prolonged stay in Paris between 1923 and 1941, partly from Roussel, but more significantly from his contacts with the music of Stravinsky and of three members of the group called 'Les Six': Milhaud, Honegger, and Poulenc. Among his debts to Stravinsky are the strong rhythms, cross-accents, metre changes, and ostinato patterns, evident in the scherzo of the First Quintet and in the first movement of the Piano Quartet. To the Parisian group he owes, in varying degrees, his use of poly-tonality (for example at the opening of the Second Quintet where the piano juxtaposes and combines arpeggiated triads of E flat and A major, the most distantly related of keys), his leaning towards baroque models, with ritornello-style reprises separated by episodic material rather than sonata-style developments, and some general touches of 'Twenties' sophistication, in the form of jazzy synco-pations and 'blues' harmony most evident in such early composi-tions as the Quartet for clarinet, horn, side-drum, and cello, of 1924, but surfacing again, with added refinement, in the Scherzo of the First Piano Quintet.

Two features of style stand out prominently. One is Martinů's oblique treatment of tonality, by which key centres are allowed to develop progressively during the course of a work or movement, with the initial key discarded by the end. In the First Quintet, for example, the opening key of F major yields to A major for the finale, while in the First Piano Quartet the first movement, in D minor, is succeeded eventually by a finale which begins in B flat and ends in G major. The other is his leaning towards a combina-tion of slow and fast sections within a single movement, as in the finale of the Second Quintet, where the opening Largo in 6/8 time, for the strings alone, is succeeded and intermingled with intense Allegro sections for the whole ensemble, with a variety of new ideas which are simply suggested rather than developed.[13] By his use of the string quartet alone at the start of this movement, Martinů shows his growing awareness of the new criteria which were beginning to govern the medium's sonority. As a violinist himself, it is for the strings that he provides, in general, his most idiomatic scoring; his piano parts, though also frequently

[13] See J. Kerman's commentary on Martinů's Second Piano Quintet, fol-lowing a performance at Princeton in 1949, in *The Music Quarterly*, (Current Chronicle), 35 (1949), 301.

independent, are usually light and open in texture, and avoid dominating the proceedings in the exaggeratedly pianistic manner to which composers of the period were not infrequently prone. His recognition of the essential dichotomy between the two 'sides' of the ensemble is nowhere better demonstrated than in the last two movements of the Piano Quartet, the first of which starts with a seventy-three-bar section for solo string trio, and the second with a twenty-two-bar Allegretto in 6/8 time, for piano alone, involving a gentle pastoral style made complex by the use of cross-rhythms in both hands.

The earliest of the American works, the Piano Quintet by Roy Harris, was completed during 1936, while the composer was teaching at the Juilliard School, and designed as a wedding gift for the pianist, Beula Duffey, whom he married in that year.[14] Its difficult, but rewarding, piano part was clearly intended as a compliment to his bride's exceptional skills. In a bold structural approach, derived more from baroque than classical models, Harris provides passacaglia and fugal treatment in the two outer movements, respectively, and encloses between them a curious section entitled 'Cadenza', in which each instrument in turn, with the exception of the second violin, is given scope for free, quasi-improvisatory, solos. The opening passacaglia is based on a symmetrical theme, with four matching phrases of seven bars each. Presented initially by the strings alone in bare octaves, it creates the impression of a measured plainchant, but contrives at the same time, with modest chromatic inflections, to embrace all twelve semitones in a non-serial manner. On the basis of this theme the composer constructs five variations of increasing elaboration, and in the process achieves a polyphonic texture of unusually rich consistency, in which the customary opposition of keyboard and strings is relatively little in evidence. In the central 'Cadenza' section, unifying references to the first movement occur at three bars after figure ①, where the viola joins the first violin with a chordal (double-stopped) version of the beginning of the passacaglia theme, and at figure ⑤, where its outline is allotted, with warmer expressive significance, to the cello. Not, however, until figure ⑦ does the piano rejoin the ensemble, at first with the strings accompanying, and then solo, in a long, unbarred, section

---

[14] See A. Mendel, 'The Quintet of Roy Harris', *Modern Music*, 17 (1939), 25.

of great brilliance which eventually leads, 'attacca', into the last movement. While thematic recall plays no significant part in the finale, it is noteworthy that the first notes of its basic fugue subject are identical to those at the start of the passacaglia theme, forming, to borrow the terminology of Renaissance sacred polyphony, a type of 'head-motif'. Altogether, the movement contains three fugue subjects, the second and third of which follow the twelve-note principle adopted in the passacaglia theme, while the first has only ten of the available semitones. No attempt is made, however, at sustained serial writing, and development of the material proceeds on broad polyphonic lines, with the use of such traditional devices as augmentation, stretto, and eventually, a climactic combination of the themes.

A gratifying example of the inter-college co-operation common in the United States at the time is provided by the fine Piano Quintet of Walter Piston, which was commissioned by the University of Michigan in 1949 shortly after the composer had been promoted to a full professorship at Harvard. Altogether more classical in structure than Harris's quintet, it has quick sonata and rondo movements flanking a central slow movement, and an overall G minor/major tonality only slightly disguised by harmony based on superimposed fourths. In style the work is lean and linear, and related most closely to that of the European neoclassicists of the time. American features are confined to occasional jazz rhythms, such as those which mark the vivid, somewhat Waltonesque, first subject of the finale (see Ex. 39). Very impres-

Ex. 39. Piston, Piano Quintet, finale

sive, in the slow movement, is the manner in which the opening theme, a sinuous melody of narrow range and uncertain tonality, and initiated by the strings alone, unfolds continuously through

an extended dynamic curve, from pianissimo to a central fortissimo climax and back, and, with a gradual simplification of the
harmony, increasingly emphasises C minor as the main key centre.

The leaning observed in Harris's work towards thematic organization in whole or partial twelve-note series, is even more
apparent in the Piano Quartet (1950) by Aaron Copland, a complex and deeply expressive work, which is notable for its imaginative scoring for the ensemble. At the opening the violin alone
presents a type of motto which links the two available forms of
the whole-tone scale, using five-note segments of each, the first
descending stepwise from B♭ to D and the second ascending from
B to G. To this there is added between the fourth and fifth notes
of the second segment—no doubt to break the otherwise too-
perfect symmetry of the combined five-note patterns—a C♮ (a
note which belongs, strictly, to the first scale segment), so as to
establish a total eleven-note pattern. Only A♮, the twelfth note of
the complete series, is omitted. Initially, the entire theme features
in a quasi-fugal exposition for the strings alone, with viola and
cello entries a major third and perfect fifth below, respectively; but
at bar 17, where the piano enters, a freely contrapuntal texture is
developed, with imitation by inversion and a chain of chords in
superimposed fourths, using only the first whole-tone segment.
Subsequently, a canonically treated second subject (from bar 29)
and a richly scored development, marked 'eloquente' and containing further canonic features, provide more sonata-like elements to
the structure. But the nearest approach to a recapitulation is a
restatement of the original motto in the final bars, a perfect fourth
higher on the piano, against held chords on the strings. And to
complete at last the full twelve-note series, the missing note (D♮,
at the higher pitch) is provided at the top of the piano part in the
final chord.

Lightly scored, apart from a few boisterous moments of climax,
the central movement is a brilliant atonal scherzo, the opening
theme of which, in the strings, has twelve notes, of which only
eleven are different, since A is repeated and B♮ omitted. However,
the serial implications of this are no more pursued here than in the
first movement. Shaped rather like a rondo with spaced repeats of
the outlines, at least, of the main theme, the movement provides a
patchwork quilt of finely-contrasted sections. At a central point
(from bar 97) whole-tone patterns return for the start of an

extended middle section (a kind of 'trio'), but give no more than a hint of cross-fertilization from the first movement. An atmosphere of calm and meditation is restored in the finale, together with a stronger feeling for tonality, centred on D flat, with a five-flat key signature to match. Three principal elements are involved (shown in Ex. 40, in differing forms, as ⓐ, ⓑ, and ⓒ): an opening section of great beauty for the three strings alone, the mildly dissonant harmony of which provides a remarkable richness of sonority without recourse to double-stoppings; a persistent three-note figure descending in whole tones on the piano, at bar 24; and a tiny fragment in leaping minor ninths, treated imitatively between the strings, at bar 34. As the movement proceeds, these themes are joined in pairs to provide contrasted expressive schemes, such as the fortissimo, 'con energia' combination of ⓐ (on the strings) and ⓑ (enlarged, on the piano) at bar 51, and the linking of ⓑ and ⓒ on the strings in a passage at bar 99, marked 'Molto calmato e molto lento' (see Ex. 40). Finally, however, it is element ⓑ which dominates the texture, gradually expanding into a five-note, descending, whole-tone scale which exactly matches, a tone lower in pitch, the opening violin phrase of the whole work.

Apart from Martinů, only Milhaud, among the many European composers who migrated, temporarily or permanently, to the United States during the 1940s, appears to have contributed significantly to the strings-and-piano chamber repertoire, with his Piano Quintet, Op. 312, in 1952 and Piano Quartet in A, Op. 417, in 1966. The second of these, a composition less remarkable for its musical substance than for its surface charm, is noteworthy for its use of a mosaic type of construction, in which major sections of the work are separated into small segments of between two and nine bars in length, and pieced together, at their eventual repetition, in a revised order. The method is well demonstrated in the lively finale. In the first half, in the course of continuous music, eight distinct texture-segments can be identified, which we may describe, in alphabetical order, as A to H; and these, in the second half, return in the entirely changed sequence F,B,E,D,C,G,A,H. At its repeat each segment retains its original pitch, but in some cases is slightly altered in texture or scoring (see Ex. 41). Interestingly, segment A, the 'official' point of recapitulation, does not reappear until most of the others have already been repeated, while segment H provides a common conclusion in each half, and thus creates an effective unifying element towards the end of the movement.

Ex. 40. Copland, Piano Quartet, finale

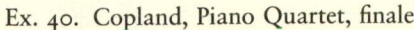

Ex. 41. Milhaud, Piano Quartet in A, Op. 417, finale

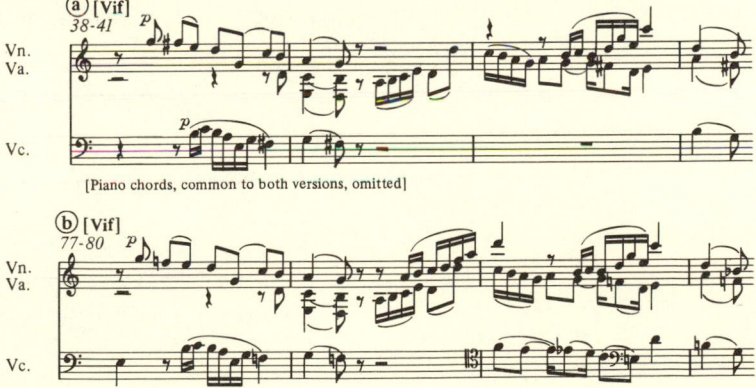

Milhaud's involvement with musical circles in the United States was considerable. After transferring there from Paris in 1940, he accepted a teaching post at Mills College, Oakland, California, and, following his return to France in 1947, not only retained this appointment for a further thirty-four years, but also formed a prolonged association with the celebrated music school at Aspen, Colorado. It was during this period that a large quantity of his chamber music was composed.

It was not, however, in the liberal environment of American academe, but, paradoxically, in the repressive cultural climate of Stalinist Russia, that the most significant contribution was made to the repertoire: the Piano Quintet, Op. 57, by Shostakovich. Completed in 1940, when the composer was 34, the work won immediate official approval, and was awarded the Stalin Prize; but at first it was by no means unanimously praised by his fellow musicians. Most severe in his criticism was Prokofiev, who decried what he saw as a lack of enterprise in the music. 'What astonishes me', he wrote, 'is that so young a composer, at the height of his powers, should be so much on his guard, and calculate every note so carefully. He never takes a single risk. One looks in vain for a daring impulse, a bold venture.'[15] It is hard to reconcile this verdict with the work itself; but no doubt, in 1940, it was difficult, even for so percipient a commentator as Prokofiev, to grasp fully the major change that had taken place in Shostakovich's style as he matured. Turning away from the ultra-modern approach he had cultivated during the late twenties and early thirties—for example, in his Second and Third Symphonies and his opera, *The Nose*—he had begun to find new scope for artistic development in a more traditionalist manner, prompted not by official state leverage (as some might have suspected) but by the realization of a pressing inner need. In the process he was able, while retaining a broad allegiance to tonality and traditional forms, to fashion for himself the clearer, but nonetheless highly individual, musical language, which he first exploited, in orchestral terms, with his Fifth Symphony, of 1937, and in the chamber field with his First String Quartet, of 1938.

The five movements of the Piano Quintet display a striking

[15] Boris Schwarz, 'Dmitry Shostakovich', *The New Grove Russian Masters*, 2, ed. Stanley Sadie (London, 1986), 187.

variety of moods, from the grandly rhetorical manner of the first section to the undisguised comic sentimentality of the finale's closing bars. Yet an outstanding degree of unity is achieved, partly through consistency of style and technique, and partly through an ingenious system of paired relationships between movements, often involving actual, though frequently veiled, thematic cross-references. The two opening movements, both set in modal forms of G minor, and linked by an 'attacca', provide a neo-baroque pairing, somewhat akin to an organ prelude and fugue. Variety of expression is provided not only between the imposing manner of the opening movement and the gently meditative style, close to late Beethoven, of the ensuing fugue, but also between the majestic outer sections of the first movement and the more prosaic 'più mosso' interlude, lightly scored like a three-part invention, enclosed between them. The scherzo, placed third, presents a complete contrast both in tonality and expression. Set in the distant key of B major, it is a boisterous dance, ironic and roughly humorous in character, with full, often somewhat crude, scoring and startling moments of mock-operatic pastiche. Its position as the centrepiece of the work, and the symmetrical arrangement of the surrounding movements, recall the scheme found in Bartók's Fifth String Quartet, completed six years earlier, which may well have served Shostakovich as a model. A further switch of mood is provided by the ensuing Intermezzo, which is once again in a baroque form, with aria-style melodic lines set over a type of free ostinato in the bass, the note patterns of which are slightly varied at each recurrence. Links with earlier movements occur at bar 41, where the piano bass brings backs the ascending scale passage at the start of the whole work; and at one bar before ⑦④, where a momentary, very beautiful, change to B major recalls the key of the scherzo. An 'attacca' link leads into the finale, the only full-blown classical sonata movement in the work, which, despite its length, lacks weight, and is designedly humorous, even gently roguish, in manner. Once again links are evident with other parts of the work: with the scherzo through a shared, even though very different, humorous intention; and with the first and second movements through a disguised recall, at figure 103, of a short pattern for the strings alone, heard earlier in bars 8−10 of the Präludium and in bars 149−52 of the Fugue. Furthermore, a calculated touch of asymmetry results from the contrasts of mode:

minor for the 'baroque' movements and major for the 'humorous dance' ones.

In the second movement Shostakovich follows an established tradition by which composers have attempted, in terms of their own musical languages, to emulate the fugal style of J. S. Bach. Examples of parallel significance are the first movement of Beethoven's C sharp minor String Quartet, the A flat minor Organ Fugue by Brahms, and the opening movement of Bartók's first String Quartet. In the Quintet, in a perfectly regular exposition by the muted strings, the first violin's modal subject in G minor (strictly, in the Aeolian mode twice transposed) is imitated a fourth below, at bar 7, by the second violin, with an 'answer' which is plagal both in melodic shape (the original opening step of a tone being reduced to a semitone), and in terms of the mode; thereafter the exposition proceeds normally with spaced subject and answer entries by the cello and viola. At each entry the theme is joined by a regular countersubject, invertible at both the octave and the twelfth, which plays a continuing role of importance, even at times (in bars 131–5, for example) as an independent theme in its own right. Wholly characteristic of Shostakovich is the way in which, after the strings have removed their mutes (from figure ㉓), a continuous flow of mildly dissonant counterpoint builds towards an elaborate central climax, involving a chromatic falling pattern on the strings, followed by a brief reminder of the opening chord of the whole work, set a semitone higher, on the piano, and a short cadenza for the cello. Noteworthy amongst the many examples of traditional fugal devices is the passage from bar 71 where a Phrygian version of the subject, initially on the cello, transfers after two bars to the second violin, while the piano supplies against it, in vividly contradictory flat keys, and with tensely bitonal effect, diminutions of the theme's first two bars (see Ex. 42). Finally, as the movement winds down to its pianissimo ending, the strings, at figure ㊶, recall, in doubled note-values, the expressive three-bar fragment heard originally in bars 8–10 of the first movement.

After the intensity achieved in the two slow movements (the Fugue and the Intermezzo), the sudden lowering of the emotional temperature in the lightweight finale comes as a major surprise. Indeed, it may well have been this movement, in particular, which aroused the somewhat intemperate observations of Prokofiev,

Ex. 42. Shostakovich, Piano Quintet, Op. 57, 2nd movement

quoted above. However, the idea that the finale of a multi-movement work should necessarily be climactic or cathartic in effect is essentially a Romantic one, subscribed to hardly at all before Beethoven's time. Shostakovich, we may conclude, was adopting an earlier, more classical, view of the finale, as a relatively undemanding movement for the entertainment of his performers and listeners—perhaps with the playful last movement of Mozart's deeply emotional String Quintet in G minor, K. 516, in mind as a specific model. Yet, even in the gaily sentimental coda to the movement, with its drowsy chromatic inversion of a subsidiary idea first heard at figure ㉝, the smile on the face of the music appears enigmatic, a Gioconda smile which, for all its gentleness, suggests that more may lie beneath the surface than its immediate charm betrays, a deeper and perhaps darker secret not readily disclosed.

6
The Relationship of Style to Scoring

NOT infrequently, in scoring for strings and piano, it is the distribution of themes and their accompaniments, and the attainment of blend and balance between the tonally non-equivalent 'sides' of the ensemble, which present the greatest technical challenges. And since scoring forms an integral part of the creative process—and is thus an important aspect of the composer's personal style—the solutions to these common problems tend naturally to be numerous and varied. The most effective types of scoring are arguably those in which themes and accompaniments can be exchanged, immediately or at long-range, between the different 'sides' of the ensemble; and those in which the accompaniments themselves, so far from being neutral patterns which simply supply harmony, reveal genuine motivic significance. These 'ideal' types of scoring, however, may be relevant only to a limited number of styles. In the case of music of a different nature—more homophonic, perhaps, or more theatrical—quite another manner of scoring may be appropriate, one concerned more with drama and rhetoric than balanced discourse, and thus involving more extended solo writing, more antiphonal interplay, and even a larger amount of straightforward doubling. It is reasonable to assume, therefore, that apart from moments of striking finesse on the one hand, or of miscalculation on the other, scoring cannot meaningfully be judged in isolation, but only in relation to the wider musical style which it serves.

By limiting the scope of this enquiry, initially, to a small number of leading works—principally the piano quintets of Schumann, Brahms, Dvořák, Franck, and Fauré (No. 2)—and by focusing particularly on the types of accompaniment and thematic exchange found in their first movements, a number of points emerge about the extent to which scoring is linked to style. In the case of the Schumann Quintet, short-scale exchange between the two 'sides' of the ensemble is almost non-existent. Instead, the composer provides a large amount of doubling which, because of the size of the string body, results in a sonorous, well-balanced texture.[1] The role of the piano is undoubtedly a dominant one; yet surprisingly perhaps, in nearly a third of the total number of bars in the first movement, it is subordinated to string solos, contributing accompaniments that are largely 'neutral' in character. Typical examples are the extended broken-chord passages in quavers in bars 35–49, and the repeated crotchet chords in bars 57–72, the patterns of which recur unaltered in the recapitulation. Accompaniments for the strings, on the other hand, are confined largely to the chords held against the piano's rapid figuration during the development section; elsewhere the instruments either double the substance of the piano part, round off the corners with isolated chords, or remain silent.

Brahms's textures, on the other hand, not only reflect the 'motivic saturation' techniques which are integral to his style, but provide also many examples of thematic exchange within the ensemble, both immediate and long-range. A typical example of his motivic approach occurs between bars 61 and 64 of the first movement of his quintet, where part of the main theme, in diminution, serves as an accompaniment on the piano to the second subject on the cello, while the violins in the following bar vie with each other in close imitation against a chordal background (see Ex. 43). Only slightly more 'neutral' is the passage in bars 23–8, where a line of broken triplets in the piano right hand creates a cogent partnership with the adjoining viola figuration, the manner of which suggests that it may have been taken directly from the first cello part in the original string quintet version. Simple accompaniments for the strings are not infrequent, but in a protean setting where the melodic emphasis shifts continually from one 'side' to the other, they are usually short-lived. And even relatively rudimentary patterns, such as the ones in bars 191–4, tend to be shaped elegantly by rests and distinctive rhythms, in order to contribute life within the texture and interest for the players. Short-scale exchanges, which are less frequent in the quintet than in the piano quartets, occur in the slow movement

---

[1] Schumann's doubling of the parts is perhaps excessive in his writing for smaller chamber groups such as the piano trio. But in his handling of larger ensembles, and of the orchestra, its validity in terms of his overall style can be confirmed by attempts to improve it—as, to some extent, Mahler discovered when rescoring the symphonies.

Ex. 43. Brahms, Piano Quintet in F minor, Op. 34, 1st movement

with a transfer of its main theme from piano to strings at bars 75 and 83, and in the finale, at bars 42 and 58, where the first subject moves from strings to piano and its semiquaver accompaniment, exactly reproduced, in the reverse direction.

Dvořák no doubt gained special insight into writing for strings from his experience as a viola player in the Provisional Theatre orchestra at Prague during the 1860s, an insight reflected in his quintet not only in the sonority of the string writing but also in the unusually generous allocation of important solos to the inner parts. Plain accompanying passages for the strings are remarkably

few in the first movement (contributing to less than a tenth of the
total number of bars), since the composer's skill in providing
countermelodies and warm interior patterns leads to what is
virtually a 'pan-melodic' texture. A fine example, with motivic
interest spread evenly through the texture, occurs from bar 181,
where the cello's high-pitched version of the first theme is supported harmonically by the viola and piano left hand, and graced
by a flowing countertheme (freely drawn from the second subject)
in the right hand, together with triplet 'heartbeats', played pianissimo, on the violins (see Ex. 44). Although the piano fulfils a

Ex. 44. Dvořák, Piano Quintet in A, Op. 81, 1st movement

generally larger accompanying role than the strings (in nearly a quarter of the total number of bars), its patterns are shaped with as much imagination as those of Brahms. To take two simple cases, there is the opening section of the movement where the plainest of chordal harmony is enlivened (in an almost apologetic avoidance of the obvious) by the combination of triplet and dotted-crotchet/quaver rhythms; and at bar 111 a passage where triplet cross-rhythms, mildly contradictory and wholly delightful for the player, give support to a richly-scored version of the second subject in the strings. Although he shares with Brahms many stylistic and technical attributes, Dvořák's approach to the problems of scoring is often broader and more colourful. Where Brahms works with subtle counter-motifs, Dvořák enriches his score with extended counter-melodies; and where Brahms creates continually varied patterns, with progressively evolving ideas, Dvořák, no doubt reflecting his national roots, prefers relatively undifferentiated paragraphs, and simple repetitions at different pitch levels, in order to preserve the grand sweep of his melodic ideas.

Our two other principal composers, Franck and Fauré, differ in style, and thus also in scoring, as much from each other as from their German and Czech counterparts. Whereas, for some composers, a strong personal orientation towards either the piano or a stringed instrument may contribute to differences in their approach to scoring, for Franck it often appears that a half-conscious leaning towards organ registration lies behind his frequent contrasts of instrumental colour, and for Fauré, the art of the song writer, behind his long cantabile string lines and flowing piano accompaniments. In the first movement of the Franck Quintet, sustained accompaniments for the piano occupy nearly a quarter of the total number of bars. Though largely 'neutral' in character, they involve a considerable range of keyboard patterns, adapted skilfully to the expressive demands of their contexts. Very striking are the different shapes chosen to provide harmony beneath separate recalls, in the strings in bare octaves, of the opening theme of the introduction—the first, from bar 193, involving low-pitched semiquaver patterns, passed from hand to hand and outlining E minor, and the second, from bar 216, rising triplet groups over widespread left-hand chords in F sharp minor. More genuinely motivic accompaniments are rare, but not entirely absent. An effective instance occurs at bar 185, where a shadowy outline of the 'motto' theme is supported, pianissimo, by the second, dotted-rhythm, phrase of the first subject proper. Against the continuously active piano part the strings, when not providing solos, are frequently confined to fragmentary roles, with long silences and isolated interventions of a somewhat indeterminate character. And at climactic points of great power, such as the final Animato section of the first movement, from bar 400, both strings and piano are allowed to stray into a type of scoring more appropriate to an orchestra than a chamber ensemble. To say that, however, is to attempt to judge the scoring independently of the style. If the quintet fails at any point to meet generally accepted chamber criteria, and this is by no means certain, it can only be the substance of the music which is at fault, not the 'inevitable' manner of its scoring.

In contrast, Fauré works with a style, and related scoring, in which moderation and delicacy of expression are the outstanding characteristics. In the first movement of his Second Quintet, long-drawn, cantabile string lines create, progressively, a closely-woven polyphonic texture, against which the role of the piano is largely accompanimental. The comparatively rare melodic contributions by the piano are confined to the right hand and, apart from the important subsidiary theme first introduced at bar 45, feature generally as single strands woven ingeniously into the string complex. The question of neutrality of content in the accompaniments hardly arises, since so much life and motivic character is to be found in each of the patterns. What is largely absent, however, is any elaborate exchange of ideas between the two 'sides' of the ensemble. Among the limited examples is the piano's lyrical melody at bar 45 which is transferred to the strings only quite late in the movement, at bar 222, where it appears, half concealed, on the first violin, in a series of imitative responses to the piano part, and at bar 279 where it eventually combines with fragments of the first theme (see themes Ⓧ and Ⓨ in Ex. 45).

The extended melodies typical of slow movements usually demand an accompaniment of relatively unvaried scoring, which moves closely in step and with matching harmonic rhythm. Examples are provided, in Schumann's quintet, by the largely neutral chords on the piano and lower strings which support the first violin's march theme throughout the the opening section; and in Brahms's, by the regular quaver patterns on the strings, each

Ex. 45. Fauré, Piano Quintet in C minor, Op. 115, 1st movement

[Piano accompaniment in semiquavers omitted]

given a gentle spring by the underlying cello pizzicato, which accompany the piano's main theme for 26 bars. Brahms, however, provides figuration which is typically more motivic than Schumann's, since it involves, continually, a shadowy augmentation of the piano's opening phrase, and as we have seen earlier, transfers the main theme to the strings at bar 83, with the original accompaniment gracefully adapted for the piano. Even more elaborate are the accompaniments in the slow movement of Dvořák's quintet. At the opening, the march-like viola theme is supported, somewhat in the manner of Schumann, by detached chords on the other strings; but an entirely new facet is introduced by the piano's shapely countertheme, which is linked precisely to that of the viola, without contrast of pace. And in the ensuing D major section, 'un pochettino piu mosso', a texture of outstanding richness is achieved by surrounding the semiquaver and triplet-quaver patterns of the first violin's main theme, not only with an upper countertheme, on the second violin, but also with pizzicato semiquavers on the lower strings and triplets deep in the piano left hand, so that, through the progress of its component parts, the whole *mélange* moves in and out of step with itself in a pattern of deeply satisfying complexity.

In the case of scherzos, the speed of the leading ideas encourages accompaniments which are either light and intermittent or designed for smooth contrast. A fine example is provided by the second movement of Fauré's C minor Quintet, where the flying semi-quavers of the piano's initial theme are supported by a repeated rhythmic pattern, played pizzicato on the lower strings, and from bar 5, by a simple rising scale on the first violin. Short-term exchanges between the two 'sides' of the ensemble are frequent— in bars 91–4 and 201–5, for example—and effective use is made of slower counterthemes, such as that on the first violin in bars 35–48. Less sophisticated, but equally effective, is Dvořák's handling of the Furiant from his quintet where, with a designedly primitive type of scoring, the accompaniments are limited mainly to simple chord patterns, repeated notes, and arpeggio figuration, such as the piano's five against three (quaver/crotchet) pattern, over static harmony, in bars 80–93, and the second violin's re-petition of the note A, on stopped and open strings alternately, from bar 100.[2] Virtually all the material proves exchangeable between the two sides, and each return of the principal subject tends to attract fresh scoring detail, together with ever richer 'placings' of its attendant countertheme, first heard on the viola from bar 9.

Increasingly evident in more modern works are two particular scoring practices: the inclusion of separate sections of some length, independently, for each 'side' of the ensemble; and the adoption of lean, even at times skeletal, writing, especially for the piano. Among the relatively few contexts in which, historically, the strings have been granted independent passages of any length, are the fugal episodes found in a number of works from the time of Weber's B flat Quartet onwards. In the majority of nineteenth-century examples, including those of Schumann, Dvořák, Taneyev, and Novák, the fugal section is placed late in the finale as a means of building up progress towards the movement's climax. It is usual for the piano to be granted eventually some share in the fugal exposition, but notable exceptions are provided by the early Piano Quintet in A minor (1855) of Saint-Saëns and the Second Quintet

---

[2] A singular example of Dvořák's use of folk colouring is provided by the third movement of his E flat Piano Quartet, Op. 87, where, from bar 78, a skilfully fashioned tremolo pattern on the piano, against pizzicato strings, creates an ef-fective imitation of a cimbalom (see also p. 68).

(1914) by Dohnányi, both of which have lengthy fugal sections entirely for strings at the start of their finales.[3]

More recent examples of this procedure include the beautiful fugal texture at the opening of Copland's Quartet, where the piano's entry, with the subject inverted in the right hand and, a bar later, in its original form in the left, is delayed until bar 17; and the second movement of the Shostakovich Quintet where the slow fugue is maintained for no less than 37 bars before the piano makes its first entry. Altogether more unusual is the technique employed in the Piano Quintet (1976) of Alfred Schnittke, in which the opening ten bars of the third movement, again for strings alone, provide three short sections of canon in progressive augmentation, recalling the practice used by Ockeghem in parts of his *Missa prolationum* of the late fifteenth-century. All four strings start from the same note and present the same theme; but each, in descending order in the score, with notes of slightly longer value, so that the second violin, viola, and cello finish their phrases, respectively, two, four, and six quavers later than the first violin (see Ex. 46). At the same time, as if in compensation, both Russian quintets begin their first movements with extended passages for the piano alone, and thus contribute further to a separation of the two 'sides' of the ensemble. An even more extreme example of

Ex. 46. Schnittke, Piano Quintet, 3rd movement

[3] A curious example of fugal writing occurs in Arensky's Piano Quintet in D major, Op. 51, of 1900, the finale of which begins with two successive fugues, based respectively on the first theme of the opening movement and on the 'vielle chanson', 'Sur la pont d'Avignon j'ai oui chanter la belle' which serves as the theme for a set of variations in the second movement. Apparently to draw attention to his contrapuntal expertise, the composer describes his movement, in parentheses, as 'In modo antico'.

separation, however, is provided by the seven-movement Piano Quintet (1963) by the Argentinian composer, Alberto Ginastera, in which the odd-numbered movements involve the full ensemble and the even-numbered ones, each entitled 'Cadenza', use smaller combinations of instruments—successively, viola and cello, two violins, and piano solo. The procedure is not unlike that found, on a more restricted scale, in the Chacony of Britten's Second String Quartet (1945), where solo cadenzas for the cello, viola, and first violin in turn, are, in a similar manner, interspersed between separate variation sections for the complete quartet.

By increasing the independence of the strings, minimizing the role of the piano, and cultivating linear writing within predominantly dissonant complexes, modern composers have radically altered many of the traditional scoring procedures. Sparse writing has represented in part a reaction, common to much twentieth-century composition, against the inflated textures of the late-Romantic period. But also it has provided a crucial means of clarification in contexts where harmonic schemes are justified more by the ear and a cultivated musical judgement than by any proven system. Some insight into the principles involved can be gained from Example 47, from the second movement (bar 249) of Copland's Piano Quartet. Distinctive sonority is provided by the use of soft, widely separated, chords on the piano to enclose the fragmentary string phrases; and by the contrast achieved between the bowed patterns, of similar rhythmic shape, on violin and muted viola, and the leaping pizzicato contributions on the cello. At the same time integration is created by two features which are common to the work as a whole: partial note-series, such as that in the recurring main theme (eleven-note with its repeated A), stated at bar 249 by the violin; and whole-tone patterns, evident in the descending piano chords in the second half of bar 250 which, together with off-beat quavers in the violin part, encompass a descending scale (given here in enharmonic equivalents), of G#, F#, E, D, C, and A#. Heard in context, the refinement of the passage is even more apparent, since it follows immediately after a climax of considerable violence which ends with the full ensemble hammering out off-beat chords of a strongly dissonant character.

Textural simplicity of a more unusual kind can be seen in the Shostakovich and Schnittke Quintets: in the former at the start of the fourth movement, where an extended first violin melody is

Ex. 47. Copland, Piano Quartet, 2nd movement

supported only by the cello, pizzicato, more than three octaves below, and at bar 97 of the scherzo, where, with apparent irony, the simplest of piano chords support a solo violin melody which appears to have drawn its inspiration from Bizet's *Carmen*; and in Schnittke's quintet, in the second movement, where a similar *faux-naif* effect is achieved by the use of a waltz-style accompaniment, shared between the lower strings and piano left hand, in support of a first violin theme based repeatedly on the notes B A C H.[4] In this case the element of burlesque is intensified when the waltz theme is set, from bar 19, as a canon five in one, with entries a bar apart, for the piano right hand and the four strings in turn, and a sharply increased level of dissonance.

Special effects are sufficiently rare in piano quartet and quintet scoring for the principal examples to stand out with some promi-

----

[4] Using German terminology where 'B' indicates B♭ and 'H', B♮.

nence. As early as 1923, Ernest Bloch, in the first of his piano quintets, introduced quartertones (indicated by diagonal dashes, up or down, before the inflected note), which provide extra colour within a work which in general is fairly conservative in style. These are used conspicuously in the ostinato figuration at the start (see p. 128) and for various decorative ideas, such as the short, distinctive, pattern in the first violin, involving accacciaturas a quartertone below C♯, at the second bar after ④, a pattern described on its recurrence in an altered form in the finale as 'like an exotic bird'. Rather surprisingly, Bloch tends to confine his use of quartertones to works in which the strings are linked with the piano, the fixed pitch of which eliminates any possibility of exact exchanges between the two sides of the ensemble—a problem also encountered in his *Méditation Hébraique* for cello and piano.

More extreme devices are not evident until well into the second half of the century. Three particular works—the piano quintets by Ginastera, Grazẏna Bacewicz (No. 2), and Schnittke—may be taken as representative of such general practice as there has been. The techniques, which are confined very largely to the strings, include the use of harmonics, *col legno* and *sul ponticello* bowing, various types of glissando and pizzicato writing, and a more extensive use of microtones. The complex string writing in Bacewicz's Second Quintet, of 1965, reflects not only her exceptional skill as a violinist, but also her interest, just awakened at the time of the work's composition, in 'new Polish' avant-garde idioms, derived largely from Lutoslawski. Notable features in the first movement include a descending glissando for both violins, at the bar before 21, marked *sul ponticello* and 'to start on any high note'; and, at the bar after ⑨, a passage for strings alone, where the first violin and viola present a rising pattern in semiquavers, *sul ponticello*, while the second violin and cello accompany with triple-stopped chords marked 'come percussione *gettato*'—'[with the bow] thrown as if percussively [against the strings]' (see Ex. 48). More remarkable still are the special effects provided in the third movement, entitled 'Scherzo fantastico', of Ginastera's Piano Quintet. With the strings muted throughout and restricted in dynamics to 'sempre *ppp* e misterioso', extensive use is made not only of high-pitched harmonics, often played tremolo and *sul ponticello*, but also of *col legno* 'drumtaps' from viola and cello, and special glissando effects, bowed and pizzicato. The piano part

Ex. 48. Bacewicz, Piano Quintet No. 2, 1st movement

is skeletal and mainly of very high pitch, and contains a section (from figure ⟨155⟩) in which a deliberately blurred result is sought by holding down the sustaining pedal for nineteen bars. The resultant texture provides a wonderfully eerie atmosphere, shot through with flitting shapes of a grotesque, even sinister, character (see Ex. 49).

Microtonal writing is employed most extensively in the first three movements of Schnittke's Quintet. Notated by means of half-drawn sharps and double-sharps to indicate notes raised by a quartertone and three-quartertone, and by blackened flats and double-flats for notes similarly lowered, the system is more complex than that of Bloch, and necessarily more challenging to

Ex. 49. Ginastera, Piano Quintet, 3rd movement

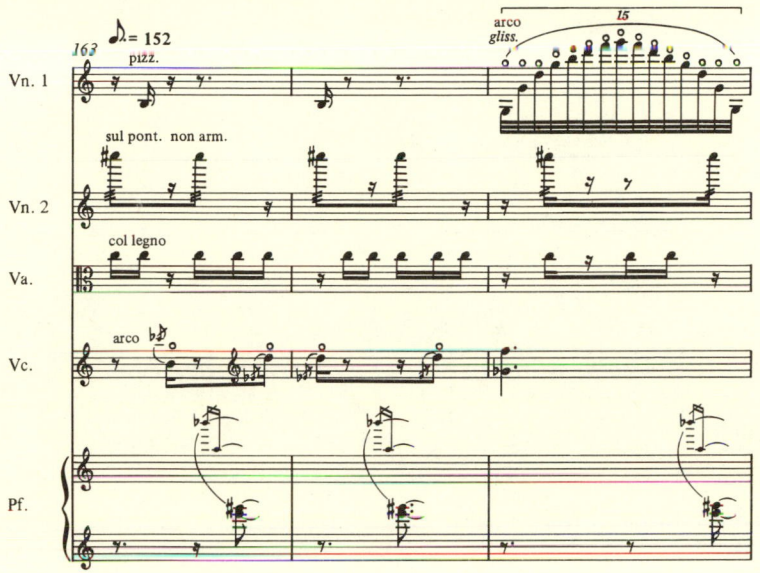

the eye of the performer. The effect produced is often of a mesmeric pattern of tiny shifting intervals, in relation to which the piano, with its fixed pitch, has either to remain silent, or to stand apart at a great distance, above and below, as shown in Example 50, from bar 50 of the first movement. Elsewhere in the work

Ex. 50. Schnittke, Piano Quintet, 1st movement

novelties of scoring are apparent chiefly in the piano part, for
example at the end of the third movement where, against a long-
held B♭, the sustaining pedal is marked to be raised and lowered
audibly five times in each of the last two bars. Also striking is the
use of 'silent touch' (*stumm anschlagen*), applied at bar 7 of the
first movement to a note cluster in the left hand. Involved are all
the semitones between A♭ and the major seventh below which,
until the sustaining pedal is released, can with skill produce the

merest shimmer of responding upper partials. Finally, there is the curious device at the end of the work's very beautiful finale, where a simple diatonic phrase in D flat major, for the right hand alone and with the sustaining pedal continuously depressed, is marked to be played 'silently, with the key-movement as virtually the only sound'—by no means an easy result to achieve.

Many of the scoring techniques identified earlier in late-nineteenth-century works have been maintained in more recent compositions—not surprisingly, perhaps, in view of the inescapable 'two-sidedness' of the media. But successive stylistic innovations have brought with them changes in emphasis. In particular, increasingly linear approaches have tended to obscure the distinction between the principal and subsidiary elements in the texture, with a consequent reduction in the scope for antiphony and the straightforward exchange of themes and accompaniments. And where special instrumental devices have been introduced, the tendency has been for the traditional relationship between style and scoring to be overturned, with the latter dictating to the former rather than the reverse.

One work of recent origin which shows outstandingly the scope that remains for novel and imaginative scoring, without recourse to extravagant effects, is the single-movement Piano Quartet (1990) by the British composer, John Casken. Acknowledging the essential 'two-sidedness' of the ensemble, and with the stated aim of 'achieving co-existence between extended singing lines and smaller, more dynamic units', the composer provides an unusually continuous piano part, full of dance rhythms and graceful arabesques, and sets it against a unified string trio texture in which fine detail abounds, but individual solos are rare. Contrast is achieved by a frequent alternation between moments of feverish activity, often involving high-pitched writing, particularly for the piano, and ones which are more passive, lower-pitched, and frequently more thinly scored. No attempt is made, however, to separate the 'sides' by giving them independent solo sections of any length. Some of these features can be seen in the passage starting at figure ㉗, in which a finely-chiselled effect results from the combination of two-part piano writing and violin pizzicati, both high pitched, and a descending scale in harmonics on the cello, with the viola, *con sordino*, 'growling' in demisemiquavers at the base of the texture (see Ex. 51).

Ex. 51. John Casken, Piano Quartet

Convincing evidence is supplied by works such as this for the continuing artistic potential of the traditional piano-and-strings media. But the tendency, already evident in the use of extravagant instrumental effects, to give greater prominence to colour than line—to prefer a 'canvas in oils' to a 'pen-and-ink drawing'—has been compounded during the present century by an increased cultivation of mixed ensembles, in which both wind and stringed instruments are combined with the piano. Though not without historical antecedents, these have established, in present-day terms, a new category of major significance; one which seems likely to provide an important, if not the most important, avenue for future development.

7
Mixed Ensembles

BEFORE the present century, composition for mixed chamber groups, with both wind and stringed instruments linked to the piano, was relatively little cultivated. Most fruitful of the available groupings was the trio—the one most precisely adapted to 'three-sided' scoring—which was preferred by leading composers to any of the larger ensembles. Its small, but eventually very impressive, repertoire includes the Trio for clarinet, viola, and piano, K. 498 of Mozart, and those in which a cello replaces the viola, by Beethoven (Op. 11), and Brahms (Op. 114), together with the latter's wonderfully effective Trio, Op. 40, for violin, horn, and piano. Combinations of greater size, usually quintets or septets, were more rarely employed, and then mainly by composers of the second rank, in works which display hybrid characteristics, often with chamber and concerto elements freely combined. The most notable examples of this second category are the Septets of Hummel and Spohr, the former (of 1816) for piano, flute, oboe, horn, viola, cello, double bass, and the latter (of 1853) for piano, flute, clarinet, horn, bassoon, violin, and cello, and on a smaller scale, the Quintet, Op. 42 (of 1893) by the Czech composer Zdeněk Fibich, for piano, clarinet, horn, violin and cello.[1] During the twentieth century, however, interest has greatly increased in this larger type of ensemble, particularly amongst leading composers, many of whom have recognized in such diverse instrumental combinations unusual scope for the exploration of new techniques, or of old techniques in new orientations.

The works chosen for survey here include some of the most important of this 'experimental' type. No regular pattern of scoring is apparent in them, except that at least one clarinet is always included, no doubt because of the instrument's wide compass and exceptionally happy blend with both the strings and the piano. In cases where two or three wind instruments are involved the usual

[1] See references to the works by Hummel, on pp. 30–1, and Fibich, on p. 70.

practice is to treat them linearly as equal contributors to the general texture, rather than as a separate group providing special melodic or harmonic colouring; and where a single wind instrument only is involved, a curb is placed on its natural tendency to fulfil a concertante role by offsetting its solo contributions with a parallel amount of accompanying material, often buried deep inside the texture.

This latter point is well illustrated by Prokofiev's Sextet in G minor, known as 'Overture on Hebrew Themes', an independent movement for clarinet, string quartet, and piano, composed in the United States, in 1919. The 'Jewish' theme at the opening, with its exotic augmented seconds, is ideally characterized by the clarinet in the lower part of its range, not only at the opening but even more so after figure ㉗, where the melody returns fragmentarily, a fifth lower in pitch, at the very bottom of the instrument's chalumeau register. Elsewhere, however, the strings are granted at least an equal share of the melodic interest, while both clarinet and piano in turn are expected to fulfil accompanying roles of greater or lesser intricacy. The true chamber character of the work is in fact confirmed as much by the careful way in which its accompanimental writing is fashioned, for all three 'sides' of the ensemble, as by the disposition of its melodic ideas. The fact that the composer later transcribed the work for orchestra need not be taken to imply that he considered the music unsuited to its original scoring, since he was much given to adapting movements or whole pieces of his own composition for new instrumental combinations. A parallel case is provided by the Andante of his first String Quartet, of 1930, which he arranged not only for string orchestra but also for piano, subsequently incorporating the latter version—together with a keyboard transcription of the Scherzo of his Sinfonietta in A, Op. 48, and several other 'borrowed' movements—into his *Six Pieces*, Op. 52, of 1930–1.

The first major chamber works with mixed scoring, from the first half of the century, to show thoroughly radical tendencies, are Schoenberg's Suite, Op. 29, of 1926 and Webern's Quartet, Op. 22, of 1930, which explore twelve-note serial techniques from totally different standpoints. Schoenberg's work, a septet scored for E flat, B flat, and bass clarinets (with flute and bassoon as alternatives to the highest and lowest instruments), together with string trio and piano, has four movements, the titles of which—

Overture, Tanzschritte (dance steps), Theme and Variations, and Gigue—suggest a general relationship with the baroque suite.[2] Standing in succession to his *Five Piano Pieces*, Op. 23, *Serenade*, Op. 24, and *Piano Suite*, Op. 25, all of 1923, and his Wind Quintet, Op. 26, of 1924, the Septet is fully serial in structure and provides one of the most stringent manifestations of the composer's theoretical principles.[3] The work's basic note series, E♭, G, F♯, A♯, D, B, C, A, G♯, E, F, C♯, evident at the start on the violin in bars 4–7, is identifiable early in each subsequent movement, most plainly in bar 6 of the Tanzschritte and bar 1 of the Gigue, where, in both cases, it is allotted to the B flat clarinet. Special colouring is derived from its initial interval of a minor sixth (E♭ falling to G) which proves, both ascending and descending, and enlarged at times to a major sixth, to be a constant contributor to later textures, and imparts a unusual degree of mellowness to them.

In common with several of his earlier works, in which he was experimenting with serial procedures, Schoenberg uses traditional forms in order to provide a familiar framework for his complex musical language. In the first movement binary sonata form is adopted, with an exposition and a much-varied recapitulation but no formal development section, since development is omnipresent. Symmetry is emphasized by the introduction of a slower section, from bar 68, in a clearly recognizable *Ländler* (slow waltz) style, with the leading theme on the viola accompanied charmingly by a conventional dance pattern on the piano, and by recalling the substance of it at bar 202, before the coda, with the principal idea transferred a minor second higher to the B flat clarinet. Binary form is used also for the second and fourth movements, in the Tanzschritte with matching pairs of themes, quick and slow, in each of its main sections, and in the largely fugal Gigue, with contrasted contrapuntal and homophonic treament of the two principal ideas in each half. Precisely balanced though the result-

---

[2] According to an outline drawn up in October 1924, the composer's original plan was for a 7-movement work with the (at that stage) largely enigmatic titles, 'Leicht (6/8) elegant, flott, bluff'; 'Jo-Jo foxtrot'; 'Fl. Kschw. [= ? Kitschweise ("kitsch style")] Walzer'; 'AS [= ? Arnold Schoenberg] Adagio'; 'J de B Muartsch Var'; 'Film Dva'; and 'Tenn Ski'. Some of these may have reflected his experience as a cabaret musician in Berlin at the beginning of the century. See preface to Philharmonia miniature score, No. 603.

[3] See E. Stein, 'Zu Schoenbergs neuer Suite, Op. 29', *Musikblätter des Anbruch*, 9 (1927), 280.

ing structures are, their clarity is not infrequently jeopardized by the intensity of the material imposed upon them. More expansive, and consequently more lucid, is the style of the third movement, a set of four variations and coda, on an extended melody, entitled 'Ännchen von Tharau', by the renowned German folk-song collector, Friedrich Silcher (1789–1860). The diatonic theme, in E major, is laid out initially on the bass clarinet, in four 5-bar phrases, with gentle accompaniment patterns, mainly of minor sixths, on the piano; and in order to preserve the central principle of construction, each note of the melody is absorbed systematically into repetitions of the fundamental series. Thus, in the case of the opening bar, the first notes of the theme, B and C♯, represent the sixth and twelfth notes of the basic note-series, while the remaining ten are incorporated into the simple chordal texture of the piano part. During the first three of the ensuing variations an outline of the original theme is preserved in a variety of scorings—successively, on the cello, piano left hand, and E flat clarinet—with added notes surrounding it to provide a consistent, but not impenetrable, disguise. While in the final variation its overall shape, though still detectable by the eye, is rendered unrecognizable to the ear through its fragmentation and complex distribution amongst the instrumental lines.

Symmetry and serial organization are again evident in the brilliantly agile Gigue, both at the opening, where a twelve-note fugue subject is answered by its exact inversion on the bass clarinet, and at the halfway point (the beginning of the second section, at bar 64) where, in reverse order, the inverted subject on the piano left hand is answered by its original form on the viola, and followed immediately, on the piano, by a combination of the theme and its augmented inversion, on left and right hands, respectively (see Ex. 52). As a means of imparting unity recalls are made at several points of themes and motifs from earlier in the work. Most readily identifiable of these are three extended returns of the 'Ännchen' theme from the third movement, introduced by the violin from bar 107, the cello from bar 117, and the B flat clarinet from bar 121.

The composer's unusual choice of instruments for the Suite no doubt reflects a desire to balance the string trio with a matching wind group, and to preserve the piano as a relatively independent element in the texture. In practice, however, the highly integrated scoring precludes the possibility of much clear opposition between

Ex. 52. Schoenberg, Suite, Op. 29, 4th movement

the groups, through either antiphonal writing or independent solos. In the rare cases where a single 'side' of the ensemble has an extended passage to itself, a link is usually provided with at least one instrument of an opposing group, in order to preserve a clear impression of textural unity. Examples are the section for string trio in bars 76–82 of the Tanzschritte, and the lengthy solo piano variation from bar 64 of the third movement, in both of which the 'linking' wind instrument is the bass clarinet. Normally, however, the composer's largely contrapuntal approach leads to a *pointilliste* style of writing for the individual instruments, in which tiny, beautifully shaped, motivic fragments are interconnected to produce a constantly shifting textural pattern, with their thematic significance indicated by *Hauptstimme* and *Nebenstimme* (leading and subsidiary part) markings.

Completed four years later, in 1930, Webern's two-movement Quartet, Op. 22, for violin, clarinet, tenor saxophone, and piano provides a skeletal texture which is in total contrast to

Schoenberg's dense scoring.[4] Conceived with the utmost economy of means, and in purely contrapuntal terms, the work focuses particularly on mirror canon techniques, in which fragmentary patterns in disjunct motion on one instrument are linked imitatively with their exact inversions on another. The underlying note-series C♯, E, F, D, D♯, B, B♭, A, A♭, F♯, C, and G, is most easily recognizable, in the first movement, from bar 6 on the saxophone; and from the start of the second movement, a fifth lower in pitch, on saxophone and clarinet, with each successive interval presented in a mirror inversion.[5] In order to impart clarity to his material, Webern, like Schoenberg, uses basic classical forms, providing in the first movement the following miniature sonata structure:

Introduction	5 bars	mirror canons for pairs of instruments
Exposition	10 bars	(with repeat sign): principal theme (two 12-note series) on the saxophone, from bar 6, with mirror canons on the accompanying instruments
Development	12 bars	mirror canons on all four instruments to bar 27, and pause
Recapitulation	10 bars	the saxophone's original 12-note theme shared between violin, clarinet, and saxophone, with mirror canons on the piano, and a sign to repeat from the start of the Development
Coda	5 bars	mirror canons, matching those of the introduction, on pairs of instruments

At the start of the exposition, the two successive versions of the 12-note series (the second a fourth lower in pitch), which form the

---

[4] Webern's sketchbooks show that the Saxophone Quartet, like his String Trio, Op. 20 and Symphony, Op. 21, was originally designed as a 3-movement work. The fact that all three works eventually had only 2 movements suggests that he was particularly attracted to the inherent symmetry of such a structure.

[5] Since so much of the structure is dependent upon mirror inversions, it is not easy to identify one form of the note-series as more 'basic' than the others. It is therefore purely for clarity's sake that the simple form provided by the saxophone from bar 6 of the first movement is taken here as fundamental.

saxophone's principal theme, are linked (in bars 10–11) by the common note G, representing their last and first notes, respectively. And in the supporting mirror patterns all twelve semitones are stated twice, in consecutive series, though not without some intermediate repetitions. Octave displacements are normal; there are virtually no instances of conjunct movement, either by a tone or semitone. And because of the fragmented style of writing which results, the variety of instrumental colour available is particularly important, since it highlights the progress of each individual, often closely intertwined, melodic line.

The second movement, which surviving sketches indicate was the first to be composed, has a more extended structure, fashioned in terms of a continual variation of the basic series, and again makes use of precisely ordered mirror canons. After an initial presentation of the inverted series on saxophone and clarinet, the violin, from bar 7, contributes a transposed version (a fourth higher) and colours it with dynamic contrasts and rapid shifts between arco and pizzicato. Even more restrained in melodic style and static in rhythm than its predecessor, the movement contains some of Weberns's most attenuated writing, particularly at the centre, in bars 69–111, where there are rarely more than two notes sounding at a time. In bars 120–8, a rather fuller texture, with increased dynamic levels, leads to a fortissimo climax; after which, in what may be seen as a rondo-like return, all four instruments participate in a recall of the series G♭, E♭, D, F, E, G♯, A, B♭, B, C♯, G, and C (first heard on the wind instruments at the start of the movement), which is itself an inverted form of the saxophone's basic theme from the first movement, transposed a fifth lower (see Ex. 53). Throughout the work the piano's role closely matches, from a melodic point of view, those of the other instruments, with the two hands adding only separate lines or individual notes to the texture. Apart from a few dyads, chordal writing is non-existent, and there is nothing to suggest that the use of the sustaining pedal would do other than destroy the crystalline clarity of the work.

Altogether less rigorous is the approach of Paul Hindemith, the leading German composer of the time, whose mature musical language though unmistakably advanced in manner, was sufficiently close to traditional practice to offer many of his contemporaries and successors a comfortable model to attempt to

Ex. 53. Webern, Saxophone Quartet, Op. 22, 2nd movement

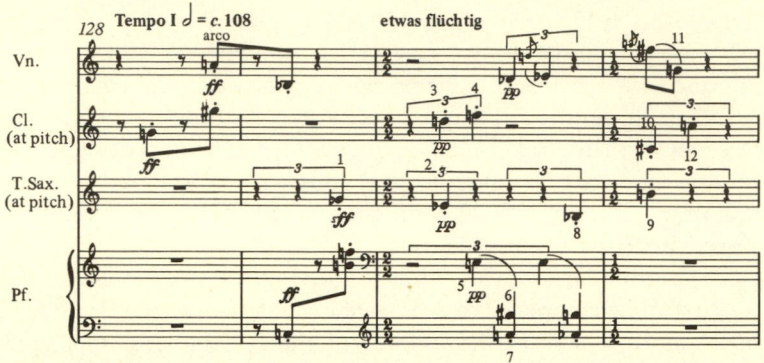

emulate. Starting as a radical experimentalist, in his early string quartets and orchestral *Kammermusik*, and in the operas *Cardillac* and *Hin und zurück*, he moved, during the 1930s, to a more temperate style, in which, following new theoretical bases (set out eventually in his *Unterweisung im Tonsatz*),[6] he gradually relaxed his starkly modernist approach in favour of a more Romantic orientation. In his exploitation of these later concepts he began at times to compose in a somewhat mechanical way, using ideas of insufficient quality to sustain the large-scale, abstract structures to which they were allied. However, claims that this departure reflected a major reduction in his creativity cannot be convincingly upheld, in view of the many brilliant successes he later achieved, not only in works on a relatively small scale, such as the witty Sonata for oboe and piano of 1938 and the elegant preludes and fugues of his *Ludus Tonalis* (1942), but also in large-scale compositions with a dramatic or programmatic motivation, such as the opera *Mathis der Maler* (1935), and the ballet *Nobilissima visione* (1938), based on the life of St Francis of Assisi.

His Quartet for clarinet, violin, cello, and piano, was composed originally in 1938 (immediately before he emigrated the United States) and reissued in a revised form in 1956. Strong in substance, it reveals a rich variety of ideas and, within the limitations of its

---

[6] Paul Hindemith, *Unterweisung im Tonsatz* (Mainz, 1937 and 1939); English edn. *The Craft of Musical Composition* (London and New York, 1942). See also C. Mason, 'Some Aspects of Hindemith's Chamber Music', *Music and Letters*, 41 1960), 150.

Ex. 54. Hindemith, Clarinet Quartet
(a) 1st movement
(b) finale

style, a masterly control of form. For the first of its three movements the composer adopts a sonata design, based on three
sharply profiled themes, each reliant in varying degrees on the
interval of a perfect fourth (see Ex. 54a). In a largely contrapuntal
setting each theme is treated in a quasi-fugal manner, with entries
on the instruments in turn, initially in delayed succession and later
telescoped into closer-knit, stretto-like, patterns. At the opening,
and in the final bars, an overall key centre of F minor/major
is established, but elsewhere wide-ranging chromaticism and a
leaning towards fourth-based harmony militate against any very
clear scheme of key contrast. As a result it is only some occasional
chordal 'signposts' which provide tonal bearings, and the structure
has to rely for its shaping largely on the character of the principal
themes and on the precise placing of points of climax. One example
of the effective use of a climax to mark a section ending is

provided by the five bars preceding figure ⑧ where, to conclude
the exposition, the piano, with semiquaver patterns drawn from
the third theme, circumnavigates in descending fourths the entire
circle of major keys, with enharmonic changes *en route* in order to
avoid an eventual plethora of double sharps.

The central slow movement, in a broad ternary form, begins
with a lyrical melody for the clarinet, supported by a closely
woven string texture and widely spread *pp* chords on the piano,
touched in with a charmingly delicate effect. In contrast the
middle section is darker and more richly scored, with low-pitched
melodic writing for the clarinet and strings, much of it in bare
octaves, set against powerful chordal and *fioritura* writing for the
piano. On the return of the first section the accompaniment to the
clarinet melody is cleverly reconstructed, with the piano developing a tiny rhythmic figure from the principal theme, to which the
strings respond antiphonally in simple dotted rhythms, played
pizzicato.

Organized in several sections in the manner of a rondo, the
finale has initial ideas of a somewhat prosaic character—at least
until reshaped in later transformations; but at seven bars after
㉞, the music is brought vividly to life by a Lebhaft (Allegro)
episode in 9/8 time, an extended section of exceptional vigour
akin to that, from figure ⑥, in the last movement of the composer's *Mathis der Maler* Symphony. Later, there occur some
unusually attractive examples of scoring: from figure ㊵, for
example, where there are ghostly exchanges, low pitched and
pianissimo, between the piano and the wind-and-strings trio; and
from six before ㊲ where the clarinet presents, in delicately
textured three-part writing, an augmented version of the opening
theme, supported by the strings alone with finely varied harmony
(see Ex. 54*b*). Towards the end, in order to create a vivid climax,
the opening theme, again in augmentation, is combined with the
energetic episode idea and underpinned by strong chords in simple
harmony on the piano. Such clarification of the harmony at points
of climax is a conspicuous feature of the composer's style. Parallel
instances occur in the first movement, at six bars after ⑤, and at
figure 14; in the slow movement during its last six bars; and in the
finale in the course of the grand peroration from figure ㊶. The
home tonic of F minor is reached in the last four bars, but, in one

of the composer's more enigmatic conclusions, with its centrality weakened by a curious emphasis on B flat major (the key of the slow movement) in the preceding bars.

Two troubled years later there appeared Messiaen's famous *Quatuor pour la Fin du Temps*. A remarkable triumph of the spirit over adversity, the work was completed during the winter of 1940−1, while the composer was confined in a prisoner-of-war camp at Görlitz in Silesia. At its first performance, given at the camp on the 15th January 1941, by the composer, as pianist, with his fellow prisoners Henri Akoka (clarinet), Jean Le Boulaire (violin), and Etienne Pasquier (cello), it is said to have been received with rapt attention by a vast audience of inmates, guards, and other officials, estimated to have numbered some five thousand. In its scoring (necessarily determined by the resources available in the camp) it resembles Hindemith's Quartet, but in all other respects is utterly different in conception. Whereas Hindemith's musical language is shaped by traditional sonata strategies, with thematic development, dynamic harmonic progressions, and key contrasts all contributing to a process of organic growth, Messiaen, whose musical roots lie 'in the anti-symphonic outlook of Debussy rather than the nineteenth-century symphonic tradition', employs altogether more static methods, with technical approaches adapted to mainly decorative ends.[7] Thus melodic and rhythmic elaboration, supported by colourful, but largely non-constructional, harmony, are often the principal factors which determine the overall shape of his music.

Nearer in structure to a suite than a sonata, with its eight relatively short, but strongly contrasted, movements, the *Quatuor* is nonetheless grandly architectural in outline. Unity is achieved, at one level, by the inspiration, plainly stated in the composer's preface, though only to a limited extent in the movement titles, which the work draws from chapter 10, verses 1−7, of the Revelation of St John the Divine, in particular from the reference to the angel who 'lifted up his hand to heaven, and sware by him that liveth for ever and ever...that there should be time no longer'. Purely musical unity, on the other hand, derives from the systematic creation of symmetries and cross-references between

---

[7] See R. Sherlaw Johnson, *Messiaen* (London, 1975; 2nd edn., 1989), 61.

the movements, together with a characteristic intermingling of birdsong—the 'antithesis of Time'. In outline the general plan of the work is as follows:

1 'Liturgie de cristal'
Full ensemble; the piano part is based on ten 'rhythmic pedals', each comprising a pattern of 17 chords in a fixed rhythm which is repeated continuously without reference to the accompanying rhythms (forming, in early Renaissance terms, a type of isorhythm); and at the same time the melodic surface provided by the initial 29 chords (corresponding to 'color' in the early music sense) is repeated five times (the last one truncated), necessarily in irregular rhythm and out of step with the keyboard's patterns. The cello has a separate melodic/rhythmic ostinato, starting in bar 2 and repeated eight and a half times; and the violin and clarinet contribute sections of 'birdsong'.

2 'Vocalise, pour l'Ange qui annonce la fin du Temps'
Full ensemble; the keyboard complex in bars 1 and 7 recurs in No. 7 at letters $\boxed{B}$ and $\boxed{E}$; and the clarinet's curved arpeggio in bar 2, in No. 3 from bar 19, and No. 4 from bar 15.

3 'Abîme des oiseaux'
Clarinet solo, with elements of 'birdsong'; the first 19 bars recur an octave lower from bar 30, and with increasing freedom, thereafter.

4 'Intermède'
Violin, clarinet, and cello, only; a scherzo not directly connected to the 'theological' scheme of the other movements, but linked to them by melodic recalls, e.g. the clarinet arpeggios from Nos. 2 and 3, and (at letter $\boxed{F}$) the opening bars of No. 6.

5 'Louange à l'Éternité de Jésus'
Cello solo with chordal piano accompaniment; in E major.

6 'Danse de la fureur, pour les sept trompettes'
Full ensemble; a monody in the sense that all four instruments play in unisons and octaves, and thus equivalent to the 3rd movement. Varied reprises occur at letters $\boxed{D}$ and $\boxed{I}$,

the second of which includes a representation of 'Les sept trompettes'.

7 'Foullis d'arcs-en-ciel, pour L'Ange qui annonce la fin du Temps'
Cello and piano (as in No. 5) for the first 12 bars, then full ensemble; variations of the first theme alternate with developments of the second; the 'second-theme' passages at letters [B] and [E] are drawn from the opening bars of the 2nd movement.

8 'Louange à l'immortalité de Jésus'
Violin solo with chordal piano accompaniment, corresponding in tempo and key (E major) to No. 5; in two halves, the second (from bar 16) identical to the first for eight bars and slightly altered thereafter.

The two slow movements for solo instrument and piano, Nos. 5 and 8, are adapted from earlier works by Messiaen. No. 5 is based on a movement entitled 'L'eau à son maximum hauteur', from *Fêtes des belles eaux* for six ondes martenot, which formed part of a *son et lumière* display at the Paris Exhibition in 1937; and No. 8 is a transposed version of the second part of a *Dyptique* for organ, dating from 1930. It is curious that the fifth movement bears no residual evidence of its origin in ondes martenot music, whereas in both the first and seventh movements the distinctive sound of the electronic instrument is clearly recalled by the difficult cello parts, involving harmonics and frequent glissandi.

While spaced repeats feature in some form in nearly all the movements, they do so with particular prominence in No. 7. Two principal themes are involved. The first, ⓐ, presented by cello and piano, comprises two phrases in matching rhythm, plus a third, slightly varied; and the second, ⓑ, for the full ensemble, starts (from bar 13) with the powerful piano passage, first heard at the opening of No. 2 (now with new support from the clarinet and strings), and is followed, at bar 17, by an important pendant, ⓒ, on the piano (see Ex. 55). Subsequently, in a series of more or less regular alternations, ⓐ reappears at bar 27, a minor third lower on the violin with an added counterpoint on the clarinet; ⓑ returns at bar 39, initially unchanged but with new developments; ⓐ occurs again, at bar 56, a tenth lower than its original pitch, on the clarinet, with a chordal accompaniment on the cello, and

Ex. 55. Messiaen, *Quatuor pour la Fin du Temps*, movement VII

[Clarinet and String parts omitted]

intervening decorative passage-work on the piano; ⓒ reappears on the piano, at bar 61, largely in its original form, but rescored; ⓐ forms a climax to the movement, from bar 82, in a fantastic manner, with trills on the three melody instruments and sweeping arpeggios on the piano, all marked 'Extatique'; and in the last four bars a further brief reference is made, fortissimo, to ⓑ. It is noteworthy that, in conformity with a basic structure outlined by the composer in his treatise *Technique de mon langage musical*, the recurrences of ⓐ take the form of variations, whereas, those of ⓑ lead always to fresh developments.[8]

Throughout the work, Messiaen's unique system of rhythmic organization—with its derivations from ancient Greek metres, Hindu decî-tâlas, medieval practice, and, in modern Western terms, Debussy and Stravinsky—is plainly in evidence. As part of a 'secret predilection' for prime numbers (particularly 5, 7, and 11), measured bar-lengths and the standard concept of 'time' are constantly subverted by free additions to, or subtractions from, the value of notes, and by the formation of unusual rhythmic patterns, often of a 'non-retrogradable' (identical both forwards and backwards) type.[9] In his preface the composer singles out No. 6, 'Danse de la fureur, pour les sept trompettes', with its use of augmented, diminished, and non-retrogradable rhythms, as a particularly characteristic example of his practice.[10] It is clear, as the composer later confirmed, and by no means entirely in jest, that the words 'pour la fin du temps', referred as much to the end of musical time in its conventional sense as to the work's underlying biblical text.[11]

Amongst the works for larger 'mixed' ensembles, particular importance attaches, for both historical and aesthetic reasons, to the three-movement Septet for clarinet, horn, bassoon, violin, viola, cello, and piano by Stravinsky. Composed in 1953, it is one of a group of compositions from the last period of his career which were coloured by a study he had made of twelve-note serial techniques, following the death of Schoenberg in 1951. By scoring the work for three winds, three strings, and piano, and by his choice of a gigue for the final movement, Stravinsky clearly intended to emulate, in homage, Schoenberg's Suite, Op. 29; and similarly, by his overall preoccupation with canonic and fugal prodecures, to express his admiration for Webern's Saxophone

---

[8] Sherlaw Johnson, *Messiaen*, 23.

[9] See D. S. Bernstein, 'Messiaen's *Quatuor pour la Fin du Temps*: an Analysis based upon Messiaen's Theory of Rhythm and his Use of Modes of Limited Transposition', Univ. of Indiana diss. 1974.

[10] See the composer's preface in the miniature score of the *Quatuor* (Durand, Paris, 1942). And for a clear and concise exposition of Messiaen's basic rhythmic practice, see Sherlaw Johnson, *Messiaen*, 32–9.

[11] In Antoine Goléa, *Rencontres avec Olivier Messiaen* (Juillard, 1960), 64.

Quartet, Op. 22.[12] There are, however, few truly serial elements in the work; it represents rather a *tour-de-force* of contrapuntal craftsmanship, in which the various patterns of notes, ordered melodically, possess hardly more 'serial' significance than those which occur naturally and repeatedly, as subjects or ostinatos in the course of traditional contrapuntal works. Partly classical and partly baroque in the forms it employs, the Septet comprises a sonata movement of regular design, followed by a passacaglia and a fugal gigue; and despite its high level of dissonance and the density of its texture, particularly in the finale, maintains a degree of tonal equilibrium throughout, centred upon A major/minor.[13]

Combined mensuration and mirror canons characterize the opening of the first movement, where the first theme, on the clarinet, is joined simultaneously by its augmentation on the bassoon, and, starting one crotchet beat later, by its inversion, again in doubled note-values, on the horn. At figure ① syncopated chords of E minor prepare for a second subject on the violin which, in Haydnesque manner, proves to be a new version of the clarinet's original theme, once again in an inverted form. At figure ③ a third, jagged, motif, with widely displaced intervals, appears on the bassoon; and this subsequently converts, at figure ④, into a short fugue subject which, worked out at considerable length, with some effective stretto entries, forms the development section (see Ex. 56). Following a regular recapitulation, the clarinet, in a markedly restrained coda, twice outlines in doubled note-values the opening four notes of its original theme, and leads down to a final chord of A major, with G♮ and D♮ added to impart distinctive colouring.

The Passacaglia is based on a pattern of sixteen notes (see Ex. 57*a*), eight of them different in pitch, which is destined to play a commanding role in the remainder of the work. Taking advantage of the range of colour provided by his mixed ensemble, the com-

---

[12] 'Of the music of this century', he declared, 'I am still most attracted by two periods of Webern: the later instrumental works [among them Op. 22] and the songs he wrote after the first twelve opus numbers and before the Trio—music which escaped the danger of the too great preciosity of the earlier pieces, and which is perhaps the richest Webern ever wrote', *Stravinsky in Conversation with Robert Craft* (London, 1962), 140.

[13] E. Stein, 'Stravinsky's Septet (1953) for Clarinet, Horn, Bassoon, Piano, Violin, Viola, and Violoncello: An Analysis', *Tempo*, 31 (Spring, 1954). See also H. Schatz, 'Igor Stravinsky: Septett', in *Melos*, 25 (1958), 60.

Ex. 56. Stravinsky, Septet, 1st movement

[Wind parts omitted]

Ex. 57. Stravinsky, Septet, 2nd movement

poser presents the note sequence, initially, in short, two-to-four note patterns on the clarinet, cello, viola, and bassoon in turn, much in the *Klangfarbenmelodie* (tone-colour melody) manner of Schoenberg and Webern. Eight variations follow, based on recurrences of the ostinato, and each decorated with contrapuntal patterns derived directly, or in some cases more obscurely, from the initial theme. In the second variation, for example, the ostinato on the cello is combined with a cantabile melodic idea on violin and viola, in close imitation, a fourth apart, using the original note sequence in an entirely new rhythmic form, together with a further countersubject on the clarinet, based on the same pattern. For the viola and clarinet contributions, transposed versions of the original series are used, a fifth and a fourth higher, respectively (see Ex. 57*b*); and in the third variation, with greater complexity, the passacaglia theme, outlined by the wind and strings, is linked with a fast moving piano part, largely in demisemiquavers, containing the basic note-pattern in each of its four standard forms—prime, inverted, retrograde, and retrograde inverted—all joined in close-knit imitations. At the end, the ostinato, in its original, plain form, is restated on the wind ensemble plus viola and cello, once again with short groups of notes split between the instruments; and with its last four notes—A, C, G♯, and A—provides the outline of a perfect cadence focused on A, and achieves thereby a limited sense of key.

The Gigue consists of four fugal sections which, following a common baroque practice, are based on the same note-pattern as the Passacaglia. A classic parallel is provided by J. S. Bach's Organ Passacaglia and Fugue in C minor, BWV 582, the 15-note Passacaglia theme of which reappears, only slightly altered, as the 'Thema Fugatum' of the ensuing section. The first part of Stravinsky's complex movement is a three-part fugue for the strings alone, with a normal exposition for viola, violin (with a dominant answer) and cello in turn, and a further subdominant ('redundant') entry on the cello, in bar 28. For the second section (from figure ㉜) the previous fugue is transferred, virtually unaltered, to the piano, and in combination with it a second fugue is added on the three wind instruments, while the strings remain silent. The subject of this added fugue, presented initially by the bassoon, is also derived strictly from the basic 16-note pattern, but with notes of double length. In the third and fourth sections a matching pair is formed to the first two. Thus, in the third, a fugue based on an inversion of the original subject is developed by the strings alone; and in the fourth, this inverted fugue is transferred exactly to the piano (as in section 2), while another fugue, with a subject based on the same inverted pattern, but pitched a major third lower and in longer note values, is added to it on the winds, the strings again remaining silent. As the two simultaneous fugues of this final section progress, extra detail is provided by wind entries using the same material in retrograde and inverse patterns, each carefully indicated in the score by the composer. The strings re-enter only in the last five bars to provide an oblique cadence in A, with the final major chord coloured by G♯, D, and B as added notes.

In the score the eight notes of different pitch in the basic (Passacaglia-cum-Fugue) theme—E, B, G, F♯, G♯, C♯, A, and C—are printed as scales, ascending or descending, above the various instrumental entries in the fugal texture. Apparently intended as an aid to analysis, these indicate the range and direction (original or inverted) of each instrument's version of the main theme, as well as the limited number of notes which are available in its entire part until, with a further fugal entry, it adopts a different pitch-range. But apart from the subject itself, no consistent pitch order is observed, so that the procedure, though greatly restricted, can hardly be described as 'serial'. If the concept is applied, however improbably, to the organ work by Bach, cited above, it transpires that a succession of seven notes of different pitch are identifiable in the Passacaglia theme, of which six (No. 7 being omitted) are present in the fugue theme, and six (with No. 2 omitted) in the countersubject which partners it. The main difference lies in the relatively unlimited pitch range and order which Bach permits himself in his additional counterpoints and episodic material, a freedom which Stravinsky appears to have been willing to forgo in the interests of an even severer form of artistic discipline.

In addition to any wish to pay homage to Schoenberg's Suite, Op. 29, Stravinsky's choice of instruments for his septet must certainly reflect a desire to emphasize the various threads in his contrapuntal textures by giving them individual colouring. This is evident particularly in his treatment of the three instrumental 'sides' in the last movement. In sections 1 and 3, where a single-theme fugue is involved, presentation by the string trio alone (apart from three-bar insertions by the wind at the end of each section) introduces an appropriate degree of homogeneity into the writing; whereas in sections 2 and 4 the two separate but interlinked complexes of the double fugues are allocated to the remaining two 'sides'—wind against piano—and, with no exchange of material between them, are thus each given totally independent colouring.

The urge to illuminate contrapuntal textures by a variety of instrumentation is evident again in two, more recent, works of British origin: the Quintet, Op. 9, for clarinet, horn, violin, cello, and piano (1967) by Hugh Wood, and the Quintet for flute, clarinet, violin, cello, and piano (1974) by Edward Harper, both single-movement compositions, but different from each other in almost every other respect. Hugh Wood's work has a sectional structure of broadly classical orientation, with spaced returns of the principal themes in the manner of a rondo. Atonal and largely contrapuntal in style, it reveals debts to Schoenberg in its partial use of twelve-note groupings and its richness of texture. Particularly noteworthy is the work's rhythmic drive, the sharp clarity of its melodic ideas and the immediacy of its expressive communication. The two principal themes—the opening idea on the horn, upward-thrusting and immensely energetic, and the appassionato cello theme at bar 91 (see Ex. 58)—give instant character to the whole movement, the second of them, in particular, providing material for a grandly rhetorical flourish on the horn in the penultimate bars. To describe the vigour and rich capacity for metamorphosis of these themes as Straussian, and to sense behind them, at some considerable distance, the friendly ghosts of *Don Juan* and *Don Quixote*, is to question neither their originality nor indeed the extraordinary technical finesse with which they are handled.

In complete contrast, the Quintet by Edward Harper is calm and unobtrusive, an impressionist sound-painting, as refined and fragile as porcelain. As a 'period-piece' of the 1970s it makes effective use of a much-cultivated avant-garde style of the time, derived from the *pointilliste* techniques of Webern and his followers, but without serial organization. Within a dynamic range which rarely rises above piano, delicate patterns of a quasi-improvisatory character are set against a slow-moving background, mainly in free rhythm and in some cases only with separate

Ex. 58. Hugh Wood, Quintet, Op. 9

timings in seconds to indicate the duration of bars. Contrast with the full ensemble is achieved in two skilfully devised dialogue passages, one for flute and clarinet, between figures ④ and ⑥, and the other for violin and cello between ⑦ and ⑨, where an 'approximate relationship' only is required in the instrumental ensemble. Relatively speaking, the most deprived contributor, as in many avant-garde works of the type, is the piano, which is granted none of the melodic interest of the other instruments and, apart from a pianissimo glissando in the bar after ⑥ (with right and left hands in contrary motion on white and black notes, respectively) and some fast chromatic scales in the final bar, is confined to widely separated single notes and chord-clusters, often bound together simply by the unreleased sustaining pedal. During the final section, from figure ⑬, a series of crescendos leads to a climax of considerable power, during which the pianist is required to control the ensemble by indicating each change of section as it occurs.

Amongst the numerous other chamber works with piano composed since the end of the Second World War, a remarkable variety of instrumental combinations is to be found, ranging in size from Klaus Huber's *Ascensus* for flute, cello, and piano (1969), through the 'Quintette à la mémoire d'Anton Webern' (1955) by Henri Pousseur, for violin, cello, clarinet, bass clarinet, and piano, to Stockhausen's *Kontrapunkte* (1952/3) (a chamber version of an earlier orchestral work), for flute, clarinet, bass clarinet, bassoon, trumpet, trombone, piano, harp, violin, and cello. In some cases, not only heavy brass, but percussion instruments also, are combined with those more traditionally found in chamber contexts. Examples with trombone include Edison Denisov's Quartet 'DSCH' (1969) and Tilo Medek's *Stadtpfeifer, Ein Schwanengesang* (1963), both of which are for clarinet, trombone, cello, and piano, and Erich Urbanner's Nonet (1981) for the even more unusual combination of flute, clarinet, bass clarinet, trombone, guitar, piano, violin, cello, and double bass. Amongst the works which include percussion, there are Niccolò Castiglione's *Tropi* (1959) for flute, clarinet, violin, cello, piano, and percussion; Alfred Schnittke's *Serenade* (1968) for clarinet, violin, double bass, percussion, and piano; and *Somakuha* (1970) for flute, oboe, harp, piano, strings, and percussion, by the veteran Japanese composer Yoritsune Matsudaira, a work which, curiously, also exists in a version for solo flute. It tends to be the fate of such compositions to be confined to the studio or workshop for performance, since their unusual scorings are difficult, for economic if for no other reasons, to accommodate in public concerts, and their technical demands are such as to debar them entirely from the amateur sphere. But this, of course, is part of the price of leadership which explorers in the field must be willing to pay.

The preoccupation with instrumental colour in these works is symptomatic not only of a desire to emphasize the individual strands in writing which is pervasively contrapuntal, but also to enhance the effect of the frankly impressionistic style found in some of the more experimental works, where dialectic has yielded place to colour effects. No consensus appears to remain about the appropriate size and composition of the ensembles to be employed in 'chamber' contexts, but there is still a steadfast adherence to the important principle of one player to a part. It is clear, however, that, with the variety of scoring and structure involved, only in the broadest sense has the idea of a consistent genre, as traditionally interpreted, been maintained. The practice of composers, in certain earlier and more stable periods, of contributing repeatedly to settled forms, in creative rivalry with their contemporaries and predecessors, has been almost exactly reversed. Nowadays, more often than not, the attraction of a particular instrumental combination or structural pattern lies simply in the fact that it has *not* previously been used. Though the enterprise shown by this latter approach is undeniable, it is hard to suppose that it necessarily makes greater demands than the former way on the originality of the composer. The result is a disruptive process which impels composers to work largely in isolation, and often with little chance of the wider communication and recognition previously available to those bound by common artistic boundaries and common aims. This is not necessarily a matter for despair. History shows that, in all the arts, the radical shifts in style and thought which periodically occur, are marked by exactly the type of fragmentation and empiricism evident today.

The great chamber forms we have been surveying, even if not already largely defunct, are unlikely to be much cultivated in the future, any more than the Viol Fantasies and Trio Sonatas of earlier times were cultivated beyond their natural life-spans. There remain, however, good reasons to suppose that a new era of classical consolidation may ensue, one perhaps that will embrace wider cultural influences than hitherto, in particular, one may suggest, those of Asian origin. Were this to happen, a recognizable tradition—and possibly even a reconstructed 'mainstream'— could continue into the future, in however changed a form. Tradition, as Stravinsky observed, 'is not simply handed down ... but undergoes a life process: it is born, grows, matures, declines, and is reborn, perhaps. These stages of growth and regrowth are always in contradiction to the stages of another concept or interpretation: true tradition lives in contradiction.'[14] The outlook,

---

[14] *Stravinsky in Conversation with Robert Craft*, 254.

he suggests, is clearly encouraging, even if the outcome remains uncertain; but as he appears to indicate by his use of the word 'perhaps', nothing can be taken for granted, not even the reliability of history as a guide.

Bibliography

ABRAHAM, G., 'The Chamber Music Works', *Borodin: the Composer and his Music* (London, 1929), 119.

ALTMANN, W., *Handbuch für Klavierquintettspieler: Wegweiser durch die Klavierquintett* (Wolfenbüttel, 1936).

—— *Handbuch für Klavierquartettspieler: Wegweiser durch die Klavierquartett* (Wolfenbüttel, 1937).

ANDERSON, E. (ed.), *The Letters of Mozart and his Family*, 2 vols. (London, 1938; 2nd edn., rev. M. Carolan and A. H. King, 1966; 3rd edn., in 1 vol., 1985).

BAILEY, K., *The Twelve-note Music of Anton Webern* (Cambridge, 1991).

BERGER, A., *Aaron Copland* (New York, 1953).

BERNSTEIN, D. S., 'Messiaen's *Quatuor pour la Fin du Temps*: an Analysis based upon Messiaen's Theory of Rhythm and his Use of Modes of Limited Transposition', University of Indiana dissertation, 1974.

BEVERIDGE, D., 'Dvořák's Piano Quintet, Op. 81: The Schumann Connection', *Chamber Music Quarterly* (Spring, 1984), 2.

BICKLEY, N. (ed. and tr.), *Brahms's Letters to and from Joachim* (London, 1914).

BOETTICHER, W., 'Das frühe Klavierquartett C-moll von Robert Schumann', *Die Musikforschung*, 31 (1978), 465.

BROCK, D. G., 'The Instrumental Music of Hummel', University of Sheffield dissertation, 1976.

BUKOFZER, M., *Music of the Classic Period, 1750–1827* (Berkeley, 1958).

BUTTERWORTH, N., 'The Piano Quartet and "The Tender Land" (1950–55)', *The Music of Aaron Copland* (London, 1985), 134.

CHISSELL, J., *Schumann*, Master Musicians (London, 1979).

—— 'Style in Bloch's Chamber Music', *Music and Letters*, 24 (1943), 30.

CHUSID, M., 'The Chamber Music of Franz Schubert', University of California, Berkeley dissertation, 1961.

CLAPHAM, J., *Dvořák* (London, 1979).

COBBETT, W. W. (ed.), *Cyclopedic Survey of Chamber Music*, 3 vols. (London, 1929; 2nd edn., 1963).

COLLES, H. C., 'Elgar's Quintet for Pianoforte and Strings, Op. 84', *Musical Times*, 60 (1919), 596.

COOPER, M., *French Music from the Death of Berlioz to the Death of Fauré* (London, 1951).

CZESLA, W., *Studien zum Finale in der Kammermusik von Johannes Brahms* (Bonn, 1968).

DEMUTH, N., 'The Chamber Music', *César Franck* (London/New York, 1949).

DEUTSCH, O. E., *Schubert: A Documentary Biography*, tr. E. Blom (London, 1946).

DEUTSCH, O. E., *Mozart: A Documentary Biography*, 2nd. edn. (London, 1966).
—— *Schubert: Thematic Catalogue of all his Works in Chronological Order* (London, 1951). Revised and enlarged German version in the *Neue Schubert Ausgabe* (Kassel, 1978).
D'INDY, V., *César Franck* (London, 1909).
DUNHILL, T., *Chamber Music: A Treatise for Students* (London, 1925).
—— 'Brahms's Quintet for Pianoforte and Strings', *Musical Times*, 72 (1931), 319.
DUNSBY, J., 'Piano Quartet in C Minor, Op. 60, First Movement', *Structural Ambiguity in Brahms: Analytical Approaches to Four Works* (Ann Arbor, 1981), 19.
EHRLICH, C., *The Piano: a History* (London, 1976; 2nd edn., 1990).
EINSTEIN, A., *Mozart: His Character, His Work* (London, 1946).
—— *Schubert* (London, 1951).
FAVRE, M., *Gabriel Faurés Kammermusik* (Zurich, 1949).
FILLION, M., 'The Accompanied Keyboard Divertimenti of Haydn and his Viennese Contemporaries, c.1750–1780, Cornell University dissertation, 1982.
FOREMAN, L., *Bax: a Composer and his Times* (London/Berkeley, 1983).
FORTUNE, N., 'The Chamber Music with Piano', in D. Arnold and N. Fortune (eds.), *The Beethoven Companion* (London, 1971), 197.
FRISCH, W., *Brahms and the Principle of the Developing Variation* (Berkeley and Los Angeles, 1984).
FUHRMANN, R., *Mannheimer Klavier-Kammermusik* (Marburg, 1963).
FULLER, D., 'Accompanied Keyboard Music', *Musical Quarterly*, 60 (1974), 222.
GAL, H., *Johannes Brahms: His Work and Personality*, tr. J. Stein (London, 1963).
GEIRINGER, K., *Brahms: His Life and Work*, tr. J. Weiner and B. Miall (London, 1936).
GOTTWALD, C., 'Friedrich Silcher und Arnold Schönberg: eine Analyse', *Beiträge zur Silcherforschung* (n.p., 1987), 75.
GROSS, E., 'The Chamber Music of Frantisek Xaver Dussek', University of Aberdeen dissertation, 1986.
GROVER, R. S., 'Chamber Music', *Ernest Chausson: The Man and his Music* (London, 1980), 188.
GUT, S., *La Musique de Chambre en France de 1870 à 1918* (Paris, 1978).
HARASZTI, E., 'La Musique de Chambre de Béla Bartók', *La Revue Musicale* xi. 2, No. 107 (1930), 114.
HENROTTE, G. A., 'The Ensemble Divertimento in Pre-classic Vienna', University of N. Carolina dissertation, 1967.
HERING, H., 'Das Klavier in der Kammermusik des 18. Jahrhundert', *Die Musikforschung*, 23 (1970), 22.
HINSON, J., *The Piano in Chamber Ensemble: An Annotated Guide* (Bloomington, Indiana, and London, 1978).

HOLETSCHEK, F., 'Das Klavier in der klassischen Kammermusik', Öster-reichische Musikzeitschrift, 13 (1958), 178.

HOLLANDER, H., 'Das Variationsprinzip in Schumanns Klavierquintett', Neue Zeitschrift für Musik, 124 (1963), 223.

HOOGERWERF, F. W., 'Tonal and Referential Aspects of the Set in Stravinsky's Septet', Journal of Musicological Research 4/1–2 (1982), 69.

HORTON, J., Mendelssohn's Chamber Music, BBC Music Guide (London, 1972).

HOWES, F., The Music of William Walton (London, 1942; 2nd edn., 1973).

HYDE, M. M., Schoenberg's Twelve-tone Harmony: the Suite Op. 29 and the Compositional Sketches (Ann Arbor, 1982).

JARDILLIER, R., La musique de chambre de César Franck (Paris, 1929).

JOHNSON, R. SHERLAW, Messiaen (London, 1975; 2nd edn., 1989).

JONES, J. B., 'The Piano and Chamber Works of Gabriel Fauré, with special reference to those works composed after 1890', University of Cambridge dissertation, 1974.

KEILLOR, F. E., 'Leontzi Honauer (1737–c.1790) and the Development of Solo and Ensemble Keyboard Music', University of Toronto dissertation, 1976.

KELLER, H., 'The Chamber Music', in H. C. Robbins Landon and Donald Mitchell (eds.), The Mozart Companion (London, 1956), 90.

—— 'Mozart — the Revolutionary Chamber Musician', The Musical Times, 122 (1981), 465.

KEMP, I., Hindemith, Oxford Studies of Composers (London, 1974).

KENNEDY, M., Portrait of Elgar (London, 1968; 3rd edn., 1987).

KERMAN, J., ['The Chamber Music of Bohuslav Martinů'] Musical Quarterly, 35 (1949), 301.

KEYS, I., Brahms Chamber Music (London, 1974).

KIDD, R. R., 'The Emergence of Chamber Music with Obbligato Keyboard in England', Acta Musicologica, 44 (1972), 122.

KING, A. H., Mozart Chamber Music (London, 1968).

KRUMMACHER, F., 'Schwierigkeiten des ästhetischen Urteils über historische Musik: Anmerkungen zu Schumanns Klavierquartett Op. 47', Festschrift Ernst Pepping zu seinem 70. Geburtstag am 12. September 1971 (Berlin, 1971), 247.

KULL, H., Dvořák's Kammermusik (Berne, 1948).

LARGE, B., Martinů (London, 1975).

LARSEN, J. P., 'Some Observations on the Development and Characteristics of Viennese Classical Instrumental Music', Studia Musicologica, 9 (1967), 131.

LAYTON, R., Franz Berwald (1796–1868): a Critical Study (London, 1959).

LONGYEAR, R. M., 'Förster': entry in New Grove Dictionary of Music and Musicians (London, 1980), 6, p. 717.

MACDONALD, M., Brahms, Master Musicians (London, 1990).

MAINE, B., 'Chamber Music' in Elgar, his Life and Works (London, 1933), 259.

MARÓTHY, J., 'Harmonic Disharmony: Shostakovich's Quintet', *Studia Musicologica*, 19 (1977), 325.

MARTYNOV, I., 'A Russian Critic on Shostakovitch's Quintet', tr. and ed. M. D. Calvocoressi, *Musical Times*, 82 (1941), 395.

MASON, C., 'Webern's Later Chamber Music', *Music and Letters*, 38 (1957), 232.

—— 'Some Aspects of Hindemith's Chamber Music', *Music and Letters*, 41 (1960), 150.

MASON, D. G., *The Chamber Music of Brahms* (New York, 1933).

MAUNDER, R., 'J. C. Bach and the Early Piano in London', *Journal of the Royal Musical Association*, 116, pt. 2 (1991), 201.

McMURTRY, B. H., 'The Music of Prince Louis Ferdinand', University of Illinois dissertation, 1972.

MENDEL, A., 'The Quintet of Roy Harris', in *Modern Music*, 17 (1939), 25.

MOSER, A., *Johannes Brahms im Briefwechsel mit Joseph Joachim*, 2 vols. (Berlin, 1908).

MUSGRAVE, M., *The Music of Brahms* (London, 1985).

NEWLIN, D., 'The Later Works of Ernest Bloch', *Musical Quarterly*, 33 (Oct. 1947), 443.

—— 'Anton von Webern: Quintet for String Quartet and Piano', *Notes*, 10 (1952–3), 674.

NEWMAN, W. S., 'Concerning the Accompanied Clavier Sonata', *Musical Quarterly*, 33 (1947), 327.

NIECKS, F., *Robert Schumann: A Supplementary and Corrective Biography* (London, 1925).

NORRIS, C., *Shostakovich: The Man and his Music* (London, 1982).

O'LEARY, J. S., 'Aspects of Structure in Webern's Quartet, Op. 22', Princeton University dissertation, 1978.

OPPEL, R., 'Über Beziehungen Beethovens zu Mozart und zu Ph. E. Bach', *Zeitschrift für Musikwissenschaft*, 5 (1922/23), 30.

ORLEDGE, R., *Gabriel Fauré* (London, 1979).

—— *Charles Koechlin (1867–1950): His Life and Works* (London, 1989).

RADCLIFFE, P., *Mendelssohn*, 3rd edn. Master Musicians (London, 1990).

REED, J., *Schubert*, Master Musicians (London, 1987).

RIEMANN, H., 'Mannheimer Kammermusik des 18. Jahrhundert', preface to *Denkmäler der Tonkunst in Bayern*, 15/6 (Leipzig, 1915).

—— 'Johann Schobert, ausgewählte Werke', preface to *Denkmäler deutsche Tonkunst*, 39 (Leipzig, 1909; repr. 1958).

ROBERTSON, A. (ed.), *Chamber Music* (London, 1957).

—— *Dvořák*, Master Musicians (London, 1941).

ROE, S. W., 'The Keyboard Music of J. C. Bach: Source Problems and Stylistic Development in the Solo and Ensemble Works', University of Oxford dissertation, 1982.

ROGER-DUCASSE, J. [Fauré] 'La Musique de Chambre', *La Révue Musicale* (1922), 60.

ROSEN, J., *Grażyna Bacewicz: Her Life and Works*, Polish Music History Series No. 2 (Los Angeles, University of South California, 1984).

SAAM, J., *Zur Geschichte des Klavierquartetts bis in die Romantik*, Sammlung Musikwissenschaftler Abhandlungen No. 9 (Strassburg, 1932).

SAWODNY, W., 'Das Klavierquintett mit Kontrabass', *Kontrabass und Bassfunktion*, ed. W. Salmen (Innsbruck, 1986).

SCHATZ, H., 'Igor Stravinsky: Septett', in *Melos*, 25 (1958), 60.

SCHMID, E. F., *Carl Philipp Emanuel Bach und seine Kammermusik* (Kassel, 1931).

SCHÖKEL, H. P., *Johann Christian Bach und die Instrumentalwerk seiner Zeit* (Wolfenbüttel, 1926).

SCHWARZ, B., 'Dmitry Shostakovich', in S. Sadie (ed.), *The New Grove Russian Masters*, 2 (London, 1986), 175.

SISMAN, E. R., 'Brahms's Slow Movements: Reinventing the "Closed" Forms', *Brahms Studies: Analytical and Historical Perspectives*, ed. G. S. Bozarth (Oxford, 1990), 79.

ŠOUREK, O., *The Chamber Music of Antonin Dvořák* (1956), an abridged version in English of *Dvořákovy skladby komorni* (Prague, 1934).

STAHMER, K. H., 'Drei Klavierquartette aus den Jahren 1875/76: Brahms, Mahler und Dvořák im Vergleich', *Hamburger Jahrbuch für Musikwissenschaft* vii, *Brahms und seiner Zeit* (Hamburg, 1984).

STAPLES, J. G., 'Six Lesser-known Piano Quintets of the Twentieth Century' [Webern, Vierne, Elgar, Martinů, Medtner, and R. L. Finney], University of Rochester dissertation, 1972.

STEIN, E., 'Zu Schoenbergs neuer Suite, Op. 29', *Musikblätter des Anbruch*, 9 (1927), 280.

—— 'Stravinsky's Septet (1953) for Clarinet, Horn, Bassoon, Piano, Violin, Viola, and Violoncello: An Analysis', *Tempo*, 31 (Spring, 1954), 7.

STERN, M. G., 'Keyboard Quartets and Quintets Published in London, 1756–1775: A Contribution to the History of Chamber Music with Obbligato Keyboard', University of Pennsylvania dissertation, 1979.

STRAVINSKY, I. and CRAFT, R., *Conversations with Igor Stravinsky* (London, 1959).

SUCKLING, N., *Fauré*, Master Musicians (London, 1951).

TAYLOR, R., *Robert Schumann: His Life and Work* (London, 1982).

TEMPERLEY, N., 'Instrumental Music in England, 1800–1850', University of Cambridge dissertation, 1959.

THAYER, A. W., *The Life of Ludwig van Beethoven*, rev. and ed. Elliott Forbes, 2 vols. (Princeton, 1964).

TOVEY, D. F., *Essays in Musical Analysis: Chamber Music* (London, 1944).

TRUSCOTT, H., 'The Importance of Hans Pfitzner: II—the Chamber Music', *Music-Survey* 1 (1947–9), 37.

TURRENTINE, H. C., *Johann Schobert and French Clavier Music from 1700 to the Revolution*, University of Iowa dissertation, 1962.

TYLER, H. M., 'The Harmonic Language of Mozart's Chamber Music, 1785–91', University of Sheffield dissertation, 1969.

ULRICH, H., *Chamber Music: The Growth and Practice of an Intimate Art* (New York, 1948).

WARD JONES, P., 'Mendelssohn's Opus 1: Bibliographical Problems of the C Minor Piano Quartet', *Sundry Sorts of Music Books: Essays on the British Library Collections Presented to O. W. Neighbour on his 70th Birthday* (London, 1993), 264.

WEBSTER, J., 'Towards a History of Viennese Chamber Music in the Early Classical Period', *Journal of the American Musicological Society*, 27 (1974), 212.

—— 'Schubert's Sonata Form and Brahms's First Maturity', II, *Nineteenth Century Music*, vol. 3, pt. 1 (July, 1979), 52.

—— 'The C Sharp Minor Version of Brahms's Op. 60', *Musical Times*, 121 (1980), 89.

WEISS, P., 'Dating the "Trout" Quintet', *Journal of the American Musicological Society*, xxxii (1979), 539.

WERBECK, W., 'E. T. A. Hoffmanns und C. M. v. Webers Kammermusik', *Mitteilungen der E. T. A. Hoffmann-Gesellschaft*, 24 (1978), 14.

WERNER-JENSEN, A., (ed.), *Reclams Kammermusikführer*, 10th edn., 1990.

WESTRUP, J. A., 'The Sketch for Schumann's Piano Quintet Op. 44', in H. Hüschen and D.-R. Moser (eds.), *Convivium Musicorum: Festschrift Wolfgang Boetticher zum sechzigsten Geburtstag* (Berlin, 1974), 367.

—— *Schubert's Chamber Music* (London, 1969).

WHITE, E. W., *Stravinsky: the Composer and his Works* (London, 1966).

WHITTALL, A., *Romantic Music* (London, 1987).

—— *Music since the First World War* (London, 1977).

WOLF, H. C., 'Die Kammermusik Paul Hindemiths', *Hindemith Jahrbuch*, 3 (1974), 80.

WOLLENBERG, S., 'Celebrating Dvořák: Affinities between Schubert and Dvořák', *Musical Times*, 132 (1991), 434.

ZIMMERSCHIED, D., 'Die Kammermusik Johann Nepomuk Hummels', University of Mainz dissertation, 1967.

Index of Principal Works

(Main references)

General Index